Empowered Health and Wellness

Dear Lynn

May the inner physician
awaken more and more
and bless your life.

Katelyn Mariah
2015

Empowered Health and Wellness

Awakening your Inner Physician

Katelyn Mariah

BFA, MA, LICSW (emirates) 2014

"No attempt should be made to cure the body without the soul. This is the great error of our day in the treatment of the human body, that physicians first separate the soul from the body."

Plato

MYSTICK CREEK
PUBLISHING

1641 Hague Ave, St. Paul, MN 55104
651-955-3673

ISBN (paperback): 978-0615664569

1 2 3 4 5 18 17 16 15 14
1st edition, September 2014

Printed in the United States of America

Editing by Marilyn King, Ph.D. –
        www.BlueLotusEditing.com
Print and eBook Formatting by Kevin Mullani –
        www.TruPublishing.com

Table of Contents

NOTE TO THE READER

This book is intended as an informational guide of healing stories and alternative healing techniques to give you a new perspective on the healing potential of the body. The healing experiences that Katelyn Mariah writes about are meant to inspire and support your own healing process. The information described herein is meant to supplement and not be a substitute for professional medical care and treatment. It should be used in conjunction with a trusted, qualified health care professional.

There is a place on the wellness continuum for both allopathic medicine and alternative medicines and modalities. The approach of this book is not to choose one at the exclusion of the other, but to use them to complement each other. Both paths are honored. Alternative medical information contained in this book is not intended as a substitute for professional care but is a reflection of the experience of the author. If you have or suspect you have a medical problem, you should consult a healthcare provider and invite them to ally with you in using all the resources available.

Katelyn Mariah BFA, MA, LICSW, has studied alternative healing and nutrition for many years; is a visionary artist, psychotherapist and a medicine woman using sound, energy and vibration; and she shares her personal experience to inspire you to treat your body in a new way. As a mental health therapist she worked with children, families and individuals for 26 years before retiring in May of 2011 so she could focus on alternative health. Katelyn Mariah is not a medical doctor and she encourages you to continue working with your doctor and use this information as an adjunct. All of the wellness stories are true and are used to inspire wellness.

INTRODUCTION TO
THE WORK OF WELLNESS

---

*"We create an illusion of the world that we call reality
and then we marinate in that."*

Elizabeth Kubler-Ross

This book is an invitation to join me on my personal wellness journey, as well as for me to share alternative techniques for achieving wellness, with the hope that it will help you expand your ideas around health and wellness. I write to support you to engage your inner healing wisdom, which I call your Inner Physician. This book is an intimate look at my personal journey, so it is vulnerable, juicy and raw at times. I have been transparent to give you an inside view into my illnesses and the struggles I encountered in the process, in hopes that it will inspire your own journey. I have had what I would call bizarre and unusual healing experiences that resulted in miracles that occurred on many levels. I want to say early in this book that I am using the words health and wellness as much as possible rather than the word "healing" because that word suggests that something is wrong that needs to be fixed. If we believe we must heal something we are always in a state of fixing, rather than a state of perfection. If on the other hand we focus on wellness that is the journey we will take. Also, healing might not mean recovering from something; instead, gaining insight and evolving from your experience might be the healing.

I had no previous thought of writing this book; it came alive on its own because it felt that my story needed to be told. I woke one morning at 4:00 and the introduction began to write itself as I lay in bed. I have resisted doing this for years, even though I knew it might be helpful to other people, because I didn't want to revisit the things that caused me such pain and I felt it would be difficult to put them all together in a book. I also wanted to leave the experiences in the past where I felt they belonged and not give them any more energy. My soul and my Inner Physician had other plans and you hold the fruits of our labor in your hands. Now I realize that in writing this book I am releasing my stories so they can help other people on journey of wellness, planting seeds of hope and health. This is by no means an exhaustive resource for alternative methods to use in healing; in fact there were so many I wanted to talk about but had to stop somewhere. I picked my favorites.

That quote by the late Elizabeth Kubler-Ross is so true. I used it because we don't have to marinate in what we think is reality; we can create a new one. My book is about doing just that from the standpoint of changing your story about health and wellness. The key thing that I want you to take away from this book, my stories and what I did to return to health and wellness is that we are a holistic system and if we pay attention it is always giving us information. What happens in our body is a reflection of what is going on in our mind and spirit and it is just a story that we can change at any point along the way. When approaching a crisis in healing it is imperative to take into consideration the mind-body-spirit connection, and to realize that our system is working in concert with The Creator, God, Source, Great Spirit or however you refer to that energy that created us.

My journey with physical illness started in 1985 with a condition that almost cost me my life. I will tell that story in a later chapter. Several chapters came after I thought I was finished with the book. One of them was Chapter 10. This gave me a unique opportunity to write about healing from within the crisis. Days after I had an accident, I was lying in bed with my arm in a cast and I realized I had one final story to tell. I began typing immediately, using one finger on my non-dominant hand to peck out the journey that you will read about later. All of the other personal stories in the book were written as reflections on the process sometime after the healing had already occurred. There are a few writings from my journals over the years woven in. Chapter 11 came about after I resisted yet again for several years. When this full circle healing happened I realized it was time to tell my stories.

Through the course of my journey to wellness I have grown to love my body for the miracle that it is. I have often pondered the fact that the human body is an incredible creation, but I never understood the depth of it until I began to experience the miraculous way that it can come back into wellness itself. Our body is a self-regulating instrument with a genetic blueprint for health. When we can step out of the way our Inner Physician, who knows much more than we do, can step in and the body will balance itself.

I am a fabulous creator and my thoughts are always becoming things. I have created magic and I have created hardship. I have learned from all of the experiences. Okay, I might have a bit of cat energy in me because I seem to have nine lives or some heavy duty guardian angels as you will see in my stories. Maybe I have had to experience the physical problems that I have endured so that I could tell my story and inspire other people to heal. I do know for sure that without my physical illnesses I would not have transformed and evolved as I have. I also believe that that if one sentence, paragraph or chapter has an impact on someone I have done my job.

I don't believe my body is unique. It is created in the very same way as everyone else's, with the same systems, blood, bones and cell structure, by the same Divine Intelligence. The only difference between us may be that I have discovered the Inner Physician. The Inner Physician is the intelligence the body has that knows what it needs in order to heal itself, return to and maintain homeostasis. The body has that wisdom innately by design; we have just lost touch with it. Let my story awaken that wisdom in you so you can experience health and well-being. In each chapter of the book you will find my personal stories of healing followed by techniques which will help you discover and begin to work with your Inner Physician.

When I started my journey back to well-being I didn't realize what I was tapping into. I put the pieces together in retrospect after experiencing seven or eight physical miracles of healing. I realized that when I focused on the reality I wanted to experience rather than the one I was experiencing, my reality shifted to wellness. I am a slow learner and a skeptic at times. Most people would have caught on after the first one! I didn't get it after the first or the second one and I kept needing proof. I thought maybe it was a fluke that my body did what it did and I couldn't grasp the idea of an inner intelligence that could bring itself back into homeostasis. If I had gotten it the first time, I would have saved myself a lot of pain and suffering, but that is okay because now I have a profound story to share, which might help you. My story wouldn't be as compelling if I had only had one miracle experience.

I understand that some of you who are reading this book might be in the depths of a physical illness and are not thinking there is much about the body that is wonderful or miraculous. You might be thinking that I don't understand what it is like to really suffer. Believe me, I do. I have suffered pain to the core of my being for long periods of time. I also understand doubt. When I was in the midst of illness, I had to take baby steps to move in the direction of health. I was filled with doubt about recovery and felt I might be stuck with my problem for the rest of my life, or that the problem might take my life and I know how frightening that is to think about. My baby steps were paying attention and celebrating the small changes that showed me I was moving in the right direction, when it would have been easier to dwell on the evidence that was in my face that said I wasn't getting better. I didn't realize at the time that I was learning and putting into action the law of attraction. Miracles happen all of the time and a miracle is really just a change in perception. Just changing the word "healing" to health and wellness is a change in perception that has a huge impact, which is why I have made a conscious effort throughout the book to use words that connote health and well-being as much as possible. There are many angles to illness and it can be explored from each angle to gain new insight.

I wrote that last sentence three times and each time I typed "many angels" when I meant to write "many angles." I feel it is important to point out that the "mistake' was significant and the angels kept pushing me to type the wrong word until I listened. I was working on this book in a coffee shop at the time and someone at the next table said, "She's like a little guardian angel." Okay, you have my attention! I am listening!

What if every illness had an angel assigned to it and we could call on that angel to help us return to perfect health? Why not? I like the idea and it deserves further exploration. If you are currently suffering from an illness of some kind, quiet your mind for a moment, call on the angel of that illness and ask for assistance. Put your illness in the angel's hands for a few minutes or days, if possible, and see what happens. Angels are playful and they usually send us signs and signals to show us which way to go. They might come in a dream, through a friend or family member or even through a stranger in a coffee shop. They speak to us in series of three of the same number. For example 444 is the signal that the angels are present. Pay attention to what shows up in your environment in the next few days. Watch for sudden flashes of insight and explore them. Get into the sense of play and let the angels fill you with joy, if only for a few days. Miracles arise out of that space.

As a culture we have lost our sense of magic and the miraculous. We need scientific proof for something to be real and accepted. So many people discount the possibility of the miraculous, the possibilities of the dream world and other worldly presences. There is an ongoing war within us between our dreams and desires and our current reality. If we can't see it, we can't believe it and if we can't believe it, it can't be real. When the war stops and we focus more energy on our desires and less on the current unwanted reality, magic will happen. I call you to the return of magic and miracles and ask you to suspend disbelief for the time being and open to the ideas in this book. There are things that we can't see, things happen that we can't understand and magic happens all of the time.

The first thing that is essential to the process of being well is letting go, and that is what you are doing when you allow the angels to take over. We have to let go of fear, disbelief, all of our preconceived notions and the doctor's voice saying you have this or that illness. I will be the first to admit that letting go of control is not easy. I used to equate letting go with giving up and I am not the kind of gal that gives up. In fact you will see evidence of my stubbornness in my stories. I was born under the sign of Aries and we can be very stubborn and impatient and if presented with a challenge we often run with it. Tell me I can't do something and I will put everything I have into proving you wrong. When doctors told me the only way was surgery or that I would have a permanent disability, I stamped my feet and protested with a resounding, "No!" This has served me by making me persistent but it has not served me when it made me hold tight to things that needed to be released. In my past I would often hold on to things way past their time of usefulness. Now I approach life with open hands.

During my health challenges I could see what happened when I couldn't let go. I would get polarized and laser focused when I was in pain and the more I focused on my pain the worse it got. When I was able to pull my focus away, even if only for a few minutes, pain would release. I learned that if I could let go and not think about my pain, movement toward wellness could happen. Many times that was not easy to do. It takes practice to stay in a centered place in the midst of pain. It takes faith to think positive thoughts when reality is saying something to the contrary, but it is positive thinking that is required most during those times.

When the first miracle occurred I was not a conscious, aware person as I am now. It has taken twenty-nine years and a lot of hard work to arrive at the consciousness I experience today. Twenty-nine years ago I was in a deep sleep consciously, in a very negative mind set, and that is partially what led to my illness in the first place. But I knew I wanted to live and that was enough for Divine Intelligence to step forward and engage my Inner Physician and my life was saved despite my state of mind. A positive state of mind is a key to well-being. The law of attraction is very common thinking these days and many people believe we create our reality with our thoughts. Positive thoughts create the kind of environment where our body, mind and spirit can thrive so that is the best place to focus your attention.

I used to be very critical of myself and my body because I bought into an artificial standard of what I thought I should look like. These negative thoughts created an environment where it was difficult for me or my body to stay in balance. How shallow we have become as a society when we use physical appearance as the standard for beauty, when real beauty has to do with our bodies being incredible creations no matter what they look like.

The fact that I can think and I can pick up a pen or sit at the computer and with my hands put those thoughts to paper and share them with the world is amazing if you think about it. The fact that I can send a thought from my brain through my body to my legs and feet so that I can move from place to place is incredible. The fact that I don't even have to think about it and my heart beats to pump life- giving blood through my veins, my lungs expand and contract to bring the air that I need, and I can eat and my body knows just what to do with it, is mind boggling. Yet we take all of this for granted and never think about it.

This is the intelligence of our body and it goes way beyond what I have already mentioned. We cut our finger and in a few days new cells have closed the wound and after a week or so you would never know there was a cut in the first place. The same is true of bones. If they break, they heal themselves so we can go back to living our lives as usual. Every five days, our whole intestinal lining is renewed. Every eleven days, our respiratory lining is replenished. Every fifteen days, all our white corpuscles are replaced; it takes 120 days for the red corpuscles. Every six months, we have a new bloodstream. Every eleven months, we have a new cell structure, and we get a new set of bones every two years. An entirely new body is recreated every seven years. That is pretty amazing. If all of that is true then all the diseased cells are replaced with healthy cells over time.

We haven't always taken this miraculous creation for granted. As babies everything was wondrous and new and our days consisted of exploring everything around us in great detail. Watch babies sometime as they discover their finger for the first time. They look at it, turn it, bend it, stick it in their mouths and move it, over and over as if they had discovered a treasure. That is exactly what they have discovered. Babies explore from the feeling level, because they haven't learned language yet, so they are not lost in the naming process and their exploration is a pure experience. Babies don't know they are looking at a "finger," they just know it is something new and exciting that has come to their attention.

The attention of my inner baby was captured when I was experiencing problems with my uterus, which I will discuss in a later chapter. I became acutely aware of what an amazing thing the female body is when I looked at a picture of the fallopian tube. The end of the fallopian tube is like a flower, which opens and closes as it transports the egg. I remember reading about that and tears came to my eyes as I said softly to myself, "It looks like a flower." The ends of the fallopian tubes, called "fimbria," collect the egg, while tiny hairlike fibers called cilia transport it towards the uterus. What happens once the egg and the sperm get to the uterus is mindblowing indeed. Now when I think of my female organs I envision a beautiful flower opening and closing and I am in awe. The body is a miracle and the temple for our soul and the more we understand this the more we will be able to tap into its innate intelligence. Most of us would agree that there are miracles in nature, but how many of us have a sense of wonder for the amazing creature that we are? Say for instance you have an issue with your lungs. If you can tap into the idea that every eleven days the lining of your lungs is replenished and visualize each new cell as healthy, think of the impact that would have on your body and the condition in your lungs.

That might seem too simplistic but it really isn't. I ask you to be open to the possibility of miracles and use the stories that I share about my own journey as a springboard to believing that you can return to health. That belief will allow your body to show you what is possible. Trust me when I say I have been a nonbeliever. I have been in the throes of pain and sickness which I thought I couldn't bear any longer. I have been discouraged and thought I would never get better and my body somehow proved me wrong each time, because somewhere inside of me there was a part of me that did believe I could get better and that seed of belief provided the ground in which it could happen. In the beginning it was only a tiny belief. It was out of desperation that I grabbed on to the hope and over time my belief in my body grew. Each time I experienced my body's healing power, my faith grew stronger. I got to the point where I trusted my body's wisdom more than I trusted the doctors. I took the risk of following the advice of my Inner Physician and my faith supported my body to do what it does naturally, return to balance.

I love my body! I haven't always been able to say that. I have been a perfectionist about my looks, my weight and my height and have often compared myself to others. Unfortunately those others are the ones we see in the media or on the movie screen or in fashion magazines and I am never going to look like them. That has been my albatross. When I began to look at my body from the standpoint of the miraculous return to well-being that I have experienced, over and over, I moved to a place of gratitude for my body that has nothing to do with the superficial. I love my body. I think it is a beautiful thing, even though I don't look like a Hollywood movie star. I am way over that shallow obsession because I know the meaning of true beauty, most of the time.

I was talking to a friend who is a yoga teacher who has been trying to get me to get into a yoga routine for years. Maybe with a little yoga I can gain a few more inches in height. During the conversation I said to my friend, "My body deserves yoga for all it has been through!" I was surprised by the comment that came from nowhere and she asked if she could quote me in her yoga classes. That spontaneous phrase sent me into a deep and rapid journey in my mind of all the miracles that have happened in my body at times of illness. I fell asleep that night with tears of gratitude in my eyes and when I woke up I began to write this book. I have learned many of my deepest lessons through physical illness and each time when the lesson is learned, my body hands me a miracle of healing. In this book I am going to share my personal healing stories and techniques I have used to support my healing in hopes that it will inspire you on your healing journey.

I have learned that well-being is our natural state, and if we stray from it we can still journey back to it. The journey begins long before disease manifests in our body and moves through the early stages of disease, through personal discovery and transformation into healing. When we are in the midst of a health crisis we are being shown that there is something that we need to take a closer look at. It might be that there is something that we need to embrace in ourselves, or forgive or pay attention to. I have found that these can be times of our greatest growth and transformation if we open up to the valuable gift that is trying to come through us. When I say gift I mean that there is always a pearl inside the pain and discomfort of our life experience. Illness is often pointing the way to the pearl that we might not have discovered any other way.

Healing can take on many forms. It doesn't always mean we will be cured of what is causing us discomfort, but it can mean that. What I think it means at a deeper level is our ability to come into balance and harmony within ourselves no matter what is going on inside and around us. Miracles happen because we see things from a new perspective and a state of harmony is created.

I want to share with you the miracles I have experienced on my journey and invite you to consider that you might do the same. The first story has to do with the animal kingdom but it illustrates the power we have to be instruments of healing energy and how we can facilitate miracles. Like I said, I am just like everyone else, I am not special and I have been the recipient of many miracles. I believe the same thing can happen to you. Use me as a catalyst to build your own belief and I will be even more grateful for having experienced the challenges that I have. If my experiences can touch just one life and open the door for a miracle, my pain and suffering have been worth it.

Some of what I write about might sound strange and unusual and even bizarre, especially some of the techniques for wellness. They came about as a direct response to the call of my soul and the requests of my Inner Physician. When we connect at that level things happen that we don't quite understand. I believe that I returned to well-being because I did listen and I did follow the guidance I received. The stories themselves might seem hard to believe but I assure you they are true stories of what happened to me. Remember to have an open mind when tapping into your Inner Physician, because sometimes its language might be foreign to us or seem silly. This inner wisdom knows better than we do what is needed for homeostasis.

Come with me on a return to wellness as we discover the Inner Physician, which is inside you waiting for you to call it to service. There are a lot of ways to tap into the Inner Physician, through dreams, meditation, art and music to name a few and I will share them with you along the way.

CHAPTER ONE

The Inner Physician

"Each patient carries his own doctor inside him. They come to us not knowing that truth. We are at our best when we give the doctor who resides within each patient a chance to go to work."

Albert Schweitzer (1875-1965)

I had independently connected with what I call the Inner Physician and was happy to find a couple of others who also found it as an active presence in each of us, even though they were past history. On the other hand I was surprised that I hadn't found more people who were aware of it who were using it in healing right now.

Albert Schweitzer, famed medical missionary, believed in the inner healing power and encouraged his fellow physicians to help their patients discover the Inner Physician. If the patient is only seen as "ill" he is cut off from his inner capacity to heal and he gives his power away to the doctor. Those who are aware that they have the innate power of the Inner Physician are empowered to work on their own behalf to find the best solution, whether it is allopathic medicine, alternative means of healing or a combination of things.

That is a completely different consciousness than the one where the doctor comes into your room and says, "I am sorry to have to tell you this but you have _____."

The blank can be any number of diseases or afflictions that are serious and/or life threatening. The first thing the patient says is, "Oh God, I have _____!" From there that becomes the story they tell to everyone. They announce it on Facebook and tell all of their friends. What happens? The moment we give our agreement to a belief, we bring it to life and now we have other people bringing it to life too! It is easy to predict what is going to happen.

There is another way and Schweitzer shared it and I discovered it on my own.

We have in our consciousness a personal doctor who is an expert on what is going on in our unique body. This consciousness is aware of what our body needs to heal itself from the disease, discomfort and illness that we encounter. The key to discovering this Inner Physician is twofold. First we must understand that miracles happen all the time and second we must learn to trust ourselves and the ability of our body to return to homeostasis. When we do that we can tap into that inner power and become partners with our health.

"Inner Healer" or "Inner Physician" or "Doctor Within" is a universal archetype that carries our highest and deepest wisdom and connection to our Source. There is no disease, illness, or physical imbalance which will not respond to the power of the Inner Physician, who is waiting for you to call it to action. People in touch with the Inner Physician are more likely to accept responsibility for their behavior and are empowered to take charge of their health. Working in concert with the Inner Physician, you take back your power and gain an ally for life. Your diet might change, you may begin an exercise routine, or seek out alternative forms of medicine because you are listening to your inner healing guide.

If all of our ideas about who we are, who we aren't and who we are supposed to be were boiled away, the nectar remaining would be a sense of personal being, a pure sense of existence, of presence, of "I am." This is our Essential Self, and its qualities, like those of the baby and the enlightened master, are pure and unrehearsed. It is the part of us that never dies. It is our uniqueness and authenticity which is not like anyone else. It is always focused on our best life and resists that which is not in our best interest. The problem is this part of us is subtle and doesn't have a language. The Essential Self is a very simple and pure sense of Presence and the Inner Physician is part of that.

The Inner Physician is active and engaged in every moment directing traffic within your body, making sure your body is working to the best of its ability within its given environment. It takes care of the body functions, with or without our help or the help of a medical professional. When we work consciously with it rather than unconsciously against it, miracles happen. We will know when it is time to work in conjunction with our doctor to heal our conditions and we will know when we should use alternative methods. Everything given to the body from the outside must first be inspected and then directed on its course by the Inner Physician so any healing that happens is due to this activity and nothing outside of you. Tapping into this energy we discover lost parts of ourselves and access higher wisdom. It gets blocked by the things we do that get in the way, such as worry, fear, control and trying to do things our way and that is why it is sometimes so hard to get well.

When the Inner Physician is engaged, a union occurs between the soul, heart, mind and Creator so that they can work together to maintain homeostasis. In partnership with the Inner Physician the power to return to wellness is strengthened. The more at ease we are at the idea the greater our chances for true health to occur. As we see the power and potential that resides within the body, many of the fears we have carried regarding our health fade away. We see that we can have an active role in reaching health and wellness and we are empowered to take steps. When you realize that the Inner Physician is working for you at all times, you will know that you are never alone in this pursuit for health and well-being. The key to self-healing is learning to trust this intuitive part of you.

We promote healing and a return to well-being in two ways. The first is with a positive attitude toward recovery and healing. This is done through a collaborative relationship between you, the physician, relatives and friends, particularly if you are involved in a serious illness. Your support team is there to help you stay focused and confident that you can recover and from that space the Inner Physician can participate to full capacity in the healing process and not be hindered by doubt in your speedy recovery.

Secondly, healing is promoted through therapeutic measures that appropriately support the healing process, be it allopathic or natural alternatives. For this to happen it is critical that the patient is an active participant in deciding what the process is and committed to undertaking it. Through this cooperative collaboration the Inner Physician is activated and fortified.

In partnership with the Inner Physician you can overcome not only minor ailments but major illness. You can call it intuition, sixth sense, clairvoyance, prophecy or Divine intervention, it doesn't really matter. What matters is that it is available to each of us, just waiting for us to call upon it. The following passage came through the connection I have been describing about six months after my uterus prolapsed. I wanted to gain understanding about what was happening in my body at the time. The meditation opened a door for me to access the Inner Physician on a deeper level. It is the best way for me to describe the experience of connecting to the Inner Physician and the wisdom of the body.

For many years, on my birthday, I did a solar return ceremony. The solar return is the time when the sun is in the same place in the natal chart that it was at the moment of your birth, when you can align with your original breath and life purpose. This meditation came when I connected a couple of hours before the breath point. The first two paragraphs are the intention that I set and what follows is the information that flowed through me. It may seem foreign to you so keep an open mind when reading. I have taken many meditative journeys so this might be more detailed than what someone who is new to the process might receive and with practice your connection with the Inner Physician and the information you receive will deepen too.

This is what I wrote and the information I received in mediation:

Today is the celebration of my birth. Forty-eight years ago I was in my mother's womb, within two hours of being born. My mother was laboring to bring me into the world. I consciously return to her womb two hours before I connect my breath again to that of my original breath.

I ask to activate the wisdom of the womb that surrounded me as a fetus. Let me remember the feeling of floating in the waters of the amniotic fluid, in the dark, moist void of my mother's womb. Bring me back in contact with the mysteries of my own womb which carries my divine blueprint and let me access wisdom that may have been left for me to discover at this time.

It is dark within this womb but my unopened eyes are able to see a radiance bouncing off the inner walls of my mother's body and it fills the space with twinkling light. It feels like a loving presence just joined me. The space in my mother can barely contain my ever-expanding human form and now she wants to release me from my dark, watery home. The walls move in and out, pressing tightly around me and pulsing me to move into this new life that I have chosen. There is stillness in this movement and I receive my final instructions before being released from the darkened space where I received nourishment and where I maintained a connection with my Primordial Mother, my home for nine months.

The softened triangular spot at the top of my head opens to receive, as the nectar of my Primordial Mother and Father pours forth into me carrying the wisdom and knowledge that will carry me through this incarnation. My body is pulsed with Godly presence that fills my cells, the wisdom keepers of my soul. I am still.

Floating in the waters of my earthly mother I know that I am love and loved. My Primordial Mother and Father speak their final words, which pour into my body through the space at that back of my head.

"Creative child of our combined essence, you are a light bearer. You carry the spark of creativity within your body. It has been encoded to activate in perfect rhythm with your divine plan. We ask that you bring your wisdom forward through word and image. The skills have been developed over many lifetimes to enable you to share this gift. You will be able to transform your challenges and experiences into images and words that will be encoded with the wisdom of the experience. Healing, transformation and remembering will occur through this creative process for not only you, but also for those who experience your work. You are an oracle. You can tap into collective knowledge and bring it forward into a form. You also have a piece of

wisdom that only you carry that must be shared. It is important now at the shift of the age that you do so.

You must know that you are loved and supported every step of the way. This is a path of lightness and darkness. Balance and wholeness will be your gift if you can do this difficult and important work. It is with great sadness that we send our daughter on her path, for we know the challenges you must face to do this work. We are grateful for this commitment you have made and we stand in waiting for your return home."

My mother's body pushes aggressively on my tiny form and I drop lower into her womb space. The force of her contractions makes me uncomfortable and anxious as I don't understand why I am suddenly experiencing pain. The soft triangle at the back of my crown pulses, drawing the wisdom from my Divine Parents into my body through my spinal column. As the contractions increase the triangle closes to contain the powerful energy I have just received. As I begin to engage within the vaginal canal of my earthly mother and descend into my new life, I forget...

When you read the passage above, did it feel familiar and unfamiliar at the same time? Did you feel a sense of comfort from the words I received from my Primordial Parents or did it seem weird to you? It is okay either way. The words were for all of us because we each have special gifts and a mission that only we can complete. The wisdom for our plan on earth is encoded in our divine blueprint and we can journey there, like I did, to gather wisdom about our health, and about our life plan.

The body speaks to us about its condition in all different languages including color, temperature, pain, numbness, chills and shivers of recognition. It speaks to us through movement as it sways, wiggles, quivers and trembles. We can sense our feelings as we get the "pit in our stomach" or the "goose bumps" that run up our arms making our hair stand up. The body gives us clues all of the time about its current state of health.

Memory is stored in the cells, in the bones and even in the hair. The DNA carries the memory of our family bloodline, which is implanted in the cells where it can be hard to locate. By developing a loving relationship with the part of us that is in dis-ease we begin the journey to health. Many times the body has become sick as a way of crying out to be noticed and cared for in those times when we are too busy focusing on other things that we forget about our body. Other times our body becomes out of balance and ill because our Essential Self is trying to teach us something that we can't learn any other way.

I have found that by dialoging with a body part in particular or with the Inner Physician you can gain tremendous insight into the cause as well as the cure for the problem. The connection is made by finding a quiet place where you will not be disturbed, quieting your mind and asking that part of your body to speak to you. When my inner thoughts are quiet and I can step out of the way the wisdom of my body comes pouring through me and I become the scribe writing down what I hear so I can contemplate it later.

I have worked with the Inner Physician and know it is real. I encourage you to drop any skepticism you might feel in the moment and just play in this energy for a while and see what happens. Put your health in the hands of the Loving Presence, who speaks through your Inner Physician, and become a partner in your health today.

I was excited to find affirmation for my belief about the Inner Physician when I was doing research to see if anyone was talking about this concept that I had discovered. No one really was but I found the following information about Paracelsus:

"Nature is the first physician, man is second."

Paracelsus [1493-1641]

At the close of the Middle Ages, Paracelsus dared to challenge the orthodox medicine of his day. With the dramatic successes he achieved through observation and deduction to discover nature's latent healing powers, Paracelsus revolutionized medicine for centuries. From my research I learned that Paracelsus was a mix of medical doctor, metaphysician and shaman so it is not surprising he would take a mind/body/spirit approach to healing. He sounds like he was way ahead of his time.

He believed that all knowledge could be discovered by intuition, searching within the human mind, because man was a microcosm of the Universe and the principles operating within the Universe operated in a corresponding way within man. Paracelsus rejected supernatural magic and instead emphasized the magical healing powers with which God had endowed Nature.

Paracelsus regarded Nature as a living organism and an expression of the One Life, and man as a microcosm of Nature and the Universe. He believed that health arose from the harmony between the microcosm (man) and the macrocosm (Nature). Man and the Universe were essentially one in nature, and there was a profound relationship between every part of Nature and its corresponding part in man. That corresponding part he called the "Inner Physician."

In his early years he had the opportunity to accompany his father, a physician, on his rounds. He learned the value of observation and became acquainted with herbs and medicinal plants. His mission was to release nature's hidden powers. He believed there was a natural remedy for illnesses and that it was humanity's responsibility to find it. Very few doctors today understand that everything we need to heal our bodies can be found in nature in the plant and mineral kingdom and have instead come to rely on profitable and unnatural pharmaceuticals.

By observing nature Paracelsus concluded that all objects in the Universe, the macrocosm, were represented in the mind of man, the microcosm, and therefore all knowledge could be discovered by searching within. Through his observations he understood that there must be an inner healing principle in living organisms which systematically combats disease. Chaos would ensue within the ailing organism if a higher organizing power were not present to intervene and take appropriate countermeasures. He applied this understanding to his practice of medicine.

The ancient physicians coined the maxim: Medicus curat – Natura sanat! Which means: the physician cures in that he prescribes the course of therapy but it is nature that heals, through the Inner Physician. In essence the physician is working in harmony with the Inner Physician, not separately.

Accordingly, the Inner Physician is a person's most important resource and greatest asset. But just as any talent can be promoted or suppressed, so can the activities of the Inner Physician be encouraged, restricted or even paralyzed, which often happens today in modern medicine. There is nothing in what we have learned that emphasizes the importance of the Inner Physician and I found little about it in my research either.

One promotes healing by means of:

1. A positive attitude toward recuperation. The physician, relatives and above all the patients themselves must strengthen confidence, belief and the will to recuperate, so that all inner powers participate in the healing process and are not hindered by any doubts of a speedy recovery. The patient must let go of the story of his illness and focus on recovery.

2. The therapeutic measures which appropriately support the natural healing process. Here the patient's active participation is critical; all therapeutic procedures undertaken by him impart new healing stimuli, which fortify the will to recuperate and thus activate the Inner Physician.

AWAKENING YOUR INNER PHYSICIAN

I want to give you a taste of what it feels like to activate the Inner Physician before we go further so you will have an experience as you read my stories. By accessing your Inner Physician, you are establishing a proactive pathway to maintaining your health and energy. This is not a substitute for medical care when called for; it is an adjunct to better health and living. Let's do an exercise to help you become familiar with your Inner Physician. Don't be concerned if you don't feel anything or you don't get profound advice the first time. It takes practice to create a strong connection. In this exercise you are summoning the power of the Inner Physician so you can begin to work with it.

Light a candle and burn incense if you wish, as a way of setting up sacred space for your work. Find a comfortable place to sit. Now relax into that comfortable place letting your body release any tension you might be holding. If you find a place of tension, focus your love and attention there as you breathe into it until it dissolves. Move to the next place and do the same until your body is relaxed and filled with love.

Breathing Exercise: Sitting upright in a chair, hands placed flat down on your thighs, begin with your breath. Imagine that you can direct your breath to the base of your spine. To enhance this exercise, try keeping the tip of your tongue on the top palette in your mouth. Through the inhale, imagine breathing up the back of your spine using your breath to clear the back of the chakras, the energy centers of the body. If you don't know where they are you can intend to clear them just by saying so and slowly breathing up the back of your spine. Now move up above your head about 4-6 inches and hold your breath for a few moments. Exhale and slowly bring your breath down the front of your body, and imagine that you are letting your breath cleanse your energy centers in the front of your body. When you reach the pelvic floor, hold your breath to the count of four, and repeat this circular breath several more times. You will feel revitalized and have cleared the energy centers around your body. You are now ready to take the journey to your Inner Physician.

Let's go to the quiet space within right now. You know where it is for you so I ask you to go there. Turn your focus inward now and ask your Inner Physician to step forward and take you on a journey to discover your body's wisdom. Ask what its name is if you would like to have something to call it. Use the first name that pops into your head. Ask for a symbol that you can use as a healing tool. If you are currently dealing with illness ask your Inner Physician to guide you to the best things to heal that disease. Now let yourself fall gently into the loving arms of your Inner

Physician, as though it is enveloping you in love, and listen.... Stay in this place until you feel complete, thank your Inner Physician and return to the room and the chair that you are sitting in.

When you return from your journey write down what you discovered. When you become more efficient at journeying you can take notes as you go but for now just be present in the journey and discover the Inner Physician and its wisdom. You might not get information during your meditation so continue to listen over the next several days. Remember that the language that the Inner Physician speaks in is often symbolic and can come as an animal that crosses your path or a conversation you overhear in the coffee shop. Be open to what is happening around you. I always find that when I ask a question my Inner Physician will find a way to answer it, maybe not right away but over the course of several days. Pay attention to the things that pop into your head as if out of nowhere. They may be important bits of information.

You will find a more extensive journey to the Inner Physician on the Mediation CD at:

www.empoweredhealthandwellness.com

CHAPTER TWO

Touched by a Hummingbird

"Hummingbird is a symbol for accomplishing that which seems impossible. Hummingbird will teach you how to find the miracle of joyful living from your own life circumstances."

Ted Andrews, Animal Speaks

This is a story about magic, mystery, miracles and the power of love. It is a story that took place several years ago but I feel it is timeless. I start with this story because it is truly miraculous. By putting the mind in the space where anything is possible, anything is possible. This is also a true story that clearly shows the possibilities we are capable of producing.

In February 1998, I went to Mexico with a group to explore the ancient ruins in the area. We stayed in a resort on the beautiful Laguna Bacalar, which is very close to the Belize border. Due to something that happened a few days before leaving, I was not in a very good place and wasn't sure how I was going to navigate my way through the trip. I needed to find a place of love and compassion inside me if I was going to be able to stay centered and enjoy myself.

The first day was designated a free day and I chose to spend it with my two new friends, James and Sandy. We joined one another in an open-air cathedral, on the grounds of our resort, to get to know one another better. I was painting a soul portrait for Sandy and James came along to watch. I had been painting soul portraits for a few years and it was a way to connect on a deeper level and uncover new information. A soul portrait is an image that I receive from the person's higher self, through connecting with my higher self and theirs. It is made up of symbols, color, numerology and images that give a message to the person receiving it. I love doing them and this was the perfect thing to be doing that day.

Two people, who were not a part of our group, walked over to where we were sitting and asked if we had seen the hummingbird on the floor on the other side of the building. Without thought, the three of us got up in unison and went over to where the very still little bird was lying on its belly. We weren't sure if it was alive or dead, so we began to do hands-on healing forming a pyramid over the bird with our hands.

Periodically we lifted our hands because the energy and heat were so intense.

This tiny, iridescent, magical green bird was close to death and barely breathing, but we couldn't give up on it. After some time, it flipped over on its back as though asking us to send energy there. Sandy examined it to see if there were any injuries. There appeared to be a break or fracture that stuck out of the neck in a bump, leaving the neck unstable. The bird was determined to live and it struggled for air. After a few minutes we decided that maybe the best we could do was to honor and support her to die. My heart broke and I started to cry at the thought of this beautiful bird dying. I picked up her limp body in my hands remembering all of the times as a child I had seen hummingbirds and wished I could hold one. Now I felt helpless as I knelt with this hummingbird dying in my hand.

I held the hummingbird, as my friends continued to send loving energy through their hands in an attempt to assist her spirit from her body and midwife its transition. I looked down at the bird and she appeared to make eye contact with me. I noticed a tiny tear running from her eye, matching the tear that was running down my cheek. Then she began to try to swallow. James said, "Did one of you make a peep sound?" Before we could answer, the bird "peeped" again. He suggested that I try letting my tears drop into the bird's beak so she could drink but I didn't think salty tears would be the best thing for a hummingbird. James remembered that he had a bottle of grapefruit drink. We fed the hummingbird the soda from the end of our fingers as her long, clear tongue reached out to savor each drop. Slowly she became livelier and soon was standing up in James' hand. Sandy and I stroked the back of her head and we noticed that the bulge we had seen earlier was gone.

Suddenly, her wings began to flap and she took flight and flew away, stopping only once to glance back at us before she disappeared from sight. We had gone into timelessness, but I realized later that we had worked on the hummingbird for more than an hour.

Hummingbird medicine is the vibration of pure love and joy and the symbol of beauty and harmony. It is also symbolic of accomplishing that which seems impossible. It is said that holding a hummingbird is rare and it will change your frequency forever. If a hummingbird rests on your hand, it shares its life force energy with you. This is the beginning of the call to awakening. And when the hummingbird opens the home of your heart, there is no turning back.

It is a rare gift to be blessed with its medicine. In an exchange of reciprocity we blessed each other. We became known as "The hummingbird healers" for the rest of the trip. I secretly knew that I was "hummingbird healed." The energy of her medicine will always be with me and I believe my frequency changed from this experience. She filled me with the energy that carried me effortlessly through what could have been a very difficult trip for a number of reasons. She came onto my path at a time when I needed to open my heart to love and compassion and that is what happened as I focused on healing her. My heart was open, compassion returned and I was in a place of love. I understand the healing power of love and intention and in my willingness to give totally to the bird in order to give it back its life, I learned that miracles could happen and this set me on a path to my healing.

I see more hummingbirds now than I ever did before, because I believe I carry their energy. They also come to me in dreams at times when I need a reminder about divine perfection and joy. One day I came home from work and noticed a tiny feather had fallen on my doorstep. I picked it up to find that it was from the tail of a tiny hummingbird, a gift from a sacred bird.

I am always awestruck by their beauty and mystery. I touched and healed a bird that was less than 4 inches long, that is often elusive, and we were both changed forever. I will never forget her or that moment when she sprang to life in front of us and flew away. It was one of those moments where there are no words – only tears of joy.

When my daughter Carrie was living in California she called me to tell me she had come across a dead hummingbird while out on a walk. It appeared to have just run into a window. She said, "What should I do, Mom?" I told her to take it home and ship it to me. It arrived a few days later, still soft and flexible as if it had just died. I dried its tiny body, wrapped it in a silk ribbon and put it in a small medicine bag as a way to always honor its medicine. You will see the hummingbird throughout this book as a reminder that what seems impossible can be possible after all.

In the next few pages we will explore hands-on healing and how it can be used.

CREATIVE TECHNIQUE
FOR WELLNESS

Healing With Hands

"To receive everything, one must open one's hands and give."

Taisen Deshimar

The hands have been used as an instrument for healing for centuries in many cultures and as part of many spiritual approaches. Most of us have heard of the spiritual term "laying on of hands" which is how healing takes place in many churches. Laying on of hands as an approach to healing might seem mystical when in fact it is a natural instinct to put our hands on someone who says they have pain somewhere. Our hands hold the energy that can heal because we are all connected to the same Source of divine energy. The term "hands-on healing" usually refers to the ability to improve the health of another person using the vital energy moving through the hands. The healer places his or her hands on the person who needs assistance and allows energy to flow into the person being treated. There are many forms of hands-on healing from simply touching a person and sending energy, to massage, energy healing, touch therapy and Reiki.

Hands-on healing is a completely natural, holistic treatment that promotes the body's ability to regenerate and heal, by intentionally activating healing energy. It works on the physical, emotional and spiritual levels, and goes where it is needed, at the level that the individual is ready to receive. Hands-on healing works with the Inner Physician, whose job it is to keep each of the tiny energy pulses that make up our physical bodies vibrating, whether we are awake, asleep, in a coma, dreaming, conscious or unconscious.

I was in Patzcuaro, Mexico during the feast of Guadalupe, which you will read about in another chapter, when I received a message from the Virgin Mary that I should begin to do hands-on healing. As I sat in the church on her feast day, I could feel the energy tingling through my hands and palms. Instinctively I placed my hands over my womb and let the energy flow, just as I had done when I helped the hummingbird, and I could feel it flowing through me. You can do the same thing right now while you sit here reading.

What actually happens during hands-on healing? Healing is all about resonance and entrainment and the frequency of vibration. When two or more things are in proximity and vibrating at different frequencies, there are three possible outcomes: The higher frequency will match the lower one, the lower one will match the higher one, or they will meet in the middle, but somehow they will come into alignment. In most cases the slower vibration will rise to match the faster frequency and that process is known as entrainment. For example, similarly tuned electric oscillators over time will match frequencies, fireflies and crickets will match with one another, women sharing a home will start menstruating at the same time, and clocks in the same room will come into alignment with each other.

Practitioners of hands-on healing learn to hold a higher vibration when they touch the body with the intention to bring the client to a higher frequency. When the lower frequency entrains with the higher frequency it can no longer hold the lower vibration of disease. Vibration releases the illness or disease and brings the person back into balance so they can return to a state of wellness. This is the energy of Love, Source or God, and it calls the cells to come back into balance. This energy from Source is more powerful than any of us knows.

Healers believe that all matter is made up of energy, therefore all living beings are able to influence the energy patterns of others. Nearly all hands-on healing methods agree that vital energy comes from outside the body, directed by the mind and amplified by the emotions. They work as a catalyst for life force energy to activate the patient's own natural healing. Some methods of hands-on healing require a talent that you are either born with or not and other methods can be learned by anyone by attending courses or experimenting on your own. Some of the healing techniques, such as qigong and Healing Touch, require years of training and discipline while other methods might be part of religious devotion and prayer.

Dr. Barbara Brennan, a world famous hands-on healer, has been researching the Human Energy Field for more than 30 years and has both healed using hands-on healing and taught thousands of others how to use their hands for healing. She created an enlightening system of healing that combines hands-on healing techniques with spiritual and psychological processes. Her system is based on the living dynamic between our energy system and its relationship to the greater world and the Creator.

Dr. Brennan says, "The Human Energy Field is the manifestation of the universal energy that is intimately involved with human life. It can be described as a luminous body that surrounds and interpenetrates the physical body, emits its own characteristic radiation and is usually called the 'aura.' The auric field is a quantum leap deeper into our personality than is our physical body. It is at this level of our being that our psychological processes take place. The Human Energy Field is the vehicle for all psychosomatic reactions. The physical body arises out of the energy field, thus an imbalance or distortion in this field will eventually cause a disease in the physical body that it governs. Therefore, healing distortions in the field will bring about healing in the physical body."

Another well-known hands-on healing technique is Healing Touch, which was developed by a nurse. Healing touch is an "energy therapy" that uses gentle hand techniques to help re-pattern the patient's energy field and accelerate healing of the body and mind. It's exciting to see more and more hospitals integrating this modality into treatment for patients.

According to the Healing Touch web site "Healing Touch is a relaxing, nurturing energy therapy. Gentle touch assists in balancing your physical, mental, emotional, and spiritual well-being. Healing Touch works with your energy field to support your natural ability to heal. It is safe for all ages and works in harmony with standard medical care."

Reiki is another hands-on healing modality that is popular today. Mikao Usui is said to have developed Reiki. He reported that he received the ability of "healing without energy depletion" after three weeks of fasting and meditating on Mount Kurama, in Japan. Reiki is a Japanese technique for stress reduction and relaxation that also promotes healing. It is administered by "laying on hands" and is based on the idea that an unseen "life force energy" flows through us and is what causes us to be alive. If one's "life force energy" is low, then we are more likely to get sick or feel stress, and if it is high, we are more capable of being happy and healthy.

The word Reiki is made of two Japanese words - Rei which means "God's Wisdom or the Higher Power" and Ki which is "life force energy." It is described as a holistic therapy which brings about healing on physical, mental, emotional and spiritual levels. Healing may occur in any or all of these domains in a single treatment, without any conscious direction by either the practitioner or the recipient, because it works on the subtle level and the energy determines where it is best needed. Reiki is a simple technique to learn according to my research. Originally it was handed down to a very small number of initiates or Masters. In the last years of the 20th Century a number of Reiki healers felt that the earth needed as much healing as possible and decided to widen the number of those initiated or "attuned" to the Reiki energy forces.

Practitioners of Reiki believe that the technique is transferred to the student during a Reiki class through an "attunement" given by a Reiki master. This attunement allows the student to tap into an unlimited supply of "life force energy" to improve one's health and enhance the quality of life. Practitioners of this healing art believe that energy flows through their palms to bring about healing and that the method can be used for self-treatment as well as treatment of others.

All of these hands-on healing techniques work in conjunction with all other medical or therapeutic techniques to relieve side effects and promote recovery. The traditional medical profession has started to accept the use of Healing Touch in their practices. It is done mostly by nurses who are already working in the hospital. This is exciting because it will open doors for other alternative methods.

I personally feel each of us has the ability to tap into the universal supply of life force energy through conscious attention and intention. Practices such as Reiki and Healing Touch enhance that ability and because the idea of tapping into life force energy is so abstract these teachings give the student something tangible to work with. Hands-on healing is enhanced when both the person doing the healing and the person receiving the healing believe it will have an impact on their problems.

Despite all of the positive results from hands-on healing there is controversy regarding its validity and skeptics feel that the only effect from energy healing is a placebo, which means the patient believed that the treatment would work and therefore it did. I believe in the power of hands-on healing because I have experienced it myself and have used it with success on clients I have worked with. If healing happens because someone put their hands on someone in an attempt to heal them, what difference does it make if it was placebo effect or the results of healing from someone's hands? I think it doesn't matter so much what caused the healing. That fact that healing occurred is what is important and if hands-on healing was an instrument I say, bravo! Healing is healing.

AWAKENING YOUR INNER PHYSICIAN

Here are a few exercises you can do to try hands-on healing for yourself.

First try this simple exercise to see if you can feel the energy in your hands. Put your palms together and rub them back and forth vigorously for a minute to create a warmth and sensitivity. Separate your hands and see if you can feel the energy which will feel like a tingling sensation. Once this happens hold your hands apart, palms facing each other, and feel what feels like a rubber ball between them. This is the life force energy that is always present in your body. By rubbing your hands together you have drawn it to the surface of your hands. You can use this technique to send energy to someone else. The more you practice this and experiment with the distance between them or maybe with a partner, you will begin to feel what energy feels like and your hands will become more sensitive to the different degrees of energy.

Try this three-step process for doing hands-on healing on someone else and have them try it on you so you can feel it too. First draw the energy into the hands to activate them. Do this by sitting quietly, in simple meditation, and focus on your breathing as you allow your body to relax. Breathe in and out through the nose, with the tip of your tongue lightly touching the roof of your mouth just behind the front teeth. Focus on keeping your breathing slow and regular, and breathe deeply into the lower abdomen. Rest the hands comfortably in your lap with palms together. Continue this breathing until you begin to notice a sensation of warmth between your palms.

Now take your hands and without physically touching the patient's body move the palms across the person's body keeping your hands 1-2 inches away as though scanning the body. When you come to an area that is injured or out of balance you will notice what seems like very hot or cold spots. Just feel the change in sensation and take note of it. The more you practice this the more you will be able to feel places that are out of balance.

Keeping your palms an inch or two away from the patient but on the spot where you feel the energy change, focus your mind on the energy from your hands. Where you find a cold spot imagine that it is warming up and where you find a hot spot imagine it is cooling down. When this healing hands method starts to work, both the healer and patient begin to feel strong physical sensations. Keep your focus on each area until you feel the energy has come back into balance.

It is important when doing this kind of work on someone else to release the energy you might have picked up during the process. When working with imbalanced energies, a healer who is not aware might absorb some of the imbalance themselves. Take care during the session to release the energy you clear from the client. This can be done by flicking your fingers away from the body or shaking your hands off during the session. Another effective way to discharge energy buildup is to wash your hands under cold water after you work on someone else.

Use the exercises as a way to strengthen your healing touch muscles and get familiar with the energy it generates.

CHAPTER THREE

Spiritual Awakening

"Only when the mind is tranquil – through self-knowledge and not through imposed self-discipline – only then, in that tranquility, in that silence, can reality come into being. It is only then that there can be bliss, that there can be creative action."

Jiddu Krishnamurti

When I was 34 years old I came down with a condition that almost took my life, but instead became a phoenix story. I had other healing experiences before this, but this one was different. If you are not familiar with the phoenix, Mediaeval Hermetists regarded the phoenix as a symbol of the accomplishment of alchemical transmutation, a process equivalent to human regeneration. Wherever it is found, the phoenix is associated with resurrection, immortality, triumph over adversity, self-renewal and that which rises out of the ashes. The phoenix does not live on fruit or flowers, but on frankincense and odoriferous gums. When it has lived five hundred years, it builds itself a nest in the branches of an oak or the top of a palm tree. It collects cinnamon and spikenard and myrrh and builds a pyre out of them on which it deposits itself to die. Once the old body is consumed by the flames, the phoenix is reborn from a worm found among the ashes and it embarks on another life.

The new, young phoenix will also live to a ripe age of 500 before it repeats the scene you have just witnessed. It is said that only one phoenix lives at a time, sweetly greeting each new day in the same way as its predecessor has and gathers wisdom as brilliant as its feathers. The magnificent phoenix of fire, with crystalline eyes, illuminates the night like a comet shooting through the sky. The bird is known to have a beautiful song which is the harmony of five notes. The song of the phoenix is said to heal the sick and give sight to the blind. When it sings, pearls fall from its beak. What a beautiful metaphor for healing the phoenix is and how exciting to know that when we are in the throes of illness we can become like the phoenix as we journey toward wellness.

I don't know if I completed my journey with as much beauty or grace as the phoenix. I can only hope I did, but it is still an awesome story, which I lived. My experience would lead me to self-renewal, triumph over adversity and transformation. I hope that my song falls like pearls upon your heart and helps with your becoming well again.

I had been married for eleven years when I arrived at a place where I was unhappy with my life and I felt trapped in an unhappy marriage. I was the mother of two young children, a nine-year-old son and four-year-old daughter, and married to a man who was chemically dependent. His addiction was so bad that my daily ritual became looking for clues that he had used the night before. I was consumed in my enabling and co-dependency. The back story to why I got sick was very traumatic and it is not necessary to share it here.

The circumstances of my life forced me to look at what I had created and find a way to change it. My resistance to making that change, in part, led to my illness. I knew three years earlier that I needed to leave but my perfectionist nature wanted to create the perfect circumstances in which to leave. I think a lot of women do that out of fear. My vision was to have my own car and a steady income so I could support my children and be able keep the house we were living in.

Envisioning it any other way was too frightening. My soul couldn't wait for my perfect plan so something higher stepped in and I ended up in a healing crisis of life or death. This is an example where a healing crisis happened so that I could learn something I wasn't learning in another way.

On a Saturday morning I woke up very sick, with severe pain in my abdomen which progressed to the point where I realized I needed medical attention. My husband was too involved in his addiction to help me in any way so I drove myself to the emergency room. I was put in a room where I waited for the doctor. The pain was so severe that I passed out on the floor while I was waiting and that is where I was when the doctor arrived. She came into the exam room and found me and scolded me for being on the floor, which I found very strange. I was surprised that the doctor didn't see the seriousness of my problem and take immediate action. She looked at me like I was crazy and told me to get up. It disappointed me that there was no compassion coming from the female doctor who I had hoped would have been an ally. A nurse and the doctor had to hold me onto the x-ray machine because I could barely stand up due to the excruciating pain.

When the results of the x-ray came back the doctor told me there was nothing wrong with me, it was just a bad case of gas, and I could go home. (I learned later that the x-ray had been misread and I was in serious trouble, but that information came months later.) I knew it wasn't "gas" but I had been taught to trust doctors and not to ask questions so I did as she said and left. This wouldn't have happened if I had been consciously connected to my Inner Physician.

I returned home experiencing pain that was worse than the pain of childbirth with severe contractions coming every two minutes throughout the weekend. Having gone through Lamaze classes when I was pregnant I thought labor breathing might help with the pain I was experiencing now. Every two minutes I had pain that was similar but worse than labor so I did labor breathing almost continuously for three days. I didn't sleep because the pain was so severe and my attempts to take warm baths were met with shooting pains down my arms as I settled myself into the water. Every time that happened I felt like I was having a heart attack. I couldn't sleep in our bedroom because my husband found my periodic, quiet moaning disturbing, so I spent most of my time sitting in a rocking chair, breathing. The rocking chair became the command post from which I directed my two young children for the next three days. By Sunday the pain was so severe that I called the emergency room again and they prescribed a laxative over the phone without seeing me. This could have been a fatal mistake had it worked. Fortunately none of my internal systems were working because they had shut down.

The following Monday, after speaking with my concerned father on the phone, I convinced my husband to take me to the doctor. When he entered the room he took one look at me and had me rushed me by ambulance to the hospital. By this time my stomach was so distended from the build-up of waste that I couldn't zip my pants and I looked like I was six months pregnant. An ultrasound revealed that I had a strangulated bowel, which is a rare condition for a person in their thirties and 95% of the people who get it die before it can be properly diagnosed. When the doctor told me I needed to have surgery, I wasn't afraid, but relieved to know something could be done to stop the pain. I had gotten to the point where I was ready to die to release myself from pain, so surgery sounded like a great option. I was in surgery for eight hours and two feet of my intestine were removed because it had died inside of me and turned black. The pain I was experiencing was the labor of my body trying to get rid of this dead organ. If the problem had been diagnosed the first day I saw a doctor, they could have saved my intestine.

This healing crisis ultimately became my wake up call. When I regained consciousness in the intensive care unit I was surprised that I was still alive. I realized that I had survived for a reason and it was clear to me that I had a mission to accomplish and it wasn't about staying in an unhappy marriage. I realized if I did stay I wouldn't survive. This was the turning point in my life when I began to rise like the phoenix from the ashes of myself. The first thing from my mouth when I saw my husband was "I want a divorce," which he thought was caused by the medication I was on, but it was the beginning of my new journey into self-discovery.

This experience cracked me open to a new level of connection with my spirituality, a new direction in my artwork and a new career direction. It was the beginning of the end of my eleven-year marriage. It was clear to me that I had stayed too long already and had almost lost my life in the process. I couldn't take that chance again.

The seriousness of my condition was brought home to me again when my family doctor and my surgeon came into my room and paced back and forth as I lay in bed with tubes coming out of practically every opening in my body. They were surprised that I had survived. The surgeon shared with me that he had taken two five gallon buckets of waste from my body and for the first time in his long career he almost got sick at the sight of that much waste and my black, dead intestine. My Inner Physician wasn't fooling around and wanted me to get the message loud and clear. Sorry doc, didn't mean to gross you out!

I was in the hospital for eight days and when I was released I moved to my mother's house because I needed someone to tend to the twelve-inch open wound in my abdomen that was stitched loosely and packed with surgical cotton. Doctors left it open so it would heal from the inside out so I would not get a staph infection. It took several months for me to recover completely. During that time I began to take the steps to leave the marriage, get on with my life and create a better life for my children.

I experienced pain and suffering through this illness and am required to take medication for the rest of my life and yet I am grateful that it happened because it woke me up to new possibilities and a new direction that I might not have discovered any other way. We each get wake up calls from spirit, some big like this one and some not so big, but they are all pushing us to become more of who we truly are so we can rise like the phoenix from life circumstances that no longer serve us. In my case I had ignored the signs along the way that were telling me something needed to change. Sometimes we need something big, a like life- threatening illness, to finally say enough is enough.

There are so many miracles that happened during this crisis, the biggest one being that the labor breathing saved my life because it shut down all of my elimination systems. I didn't go to the bathroom for three days, nor was I hungry or thirsty. I had tapped into my inner wisdom and my Inner Physician had closed down shop so my body would stay alive. If my systems hadn't shut down the laxative that was prescribed by a doctor over the weekend would have killed me because my intestines would have exploded. Like the phoenix my body began to consume itself to rid me of the toxic organ and the pain became like my fire.

What I believe I had tapped into by doing the breathing was not unlike techniques used by yogis to shut down their systems so they wouldn't have to eat, sleep or feel the air temperature. They use breathing and meditation to slow down their heart rate so it is barely detectable. Ancient yogis knew there was a link between our different brain structures and the breath. The hypothalamus instructs the autonomic nervous system to regulate things like breathing, heart rate, digestion, and blood pressure and it also tells the pituitary gland to send out hormones regulating growth and metabolism. They took this knowledge a step further and developed an extensive system of breathing methods and techniques. I had no idea when I began to do labor breathing for pain control that it would be the very thing that would save my life. Breathing is one of the few autonomic functions of the body that we may also control and the more experienced yogis and yoginis learned to control heart rate, blood pressure, skin temperature, and other functions previously believed to be autonomic using the breath. There was no way I would have known how to do this without Divine intervention. My Inner Physician had gotten my attention!

Let's explore breathing, the breath and ways to use it for wellness.

CREATIVE TECHNIQUE
FOR WELLNESS

The Power of the Breath

"For breath is life, and if you breathe well you will live long on earth."

Sanskrit Proverb

"Nearly every physical problem is accompanied by a disturbance of breathing. But which comes first?"

Hans Weller, MD

"All chronic pain, suffering and diseases are caused from a lack of oxygen at the cell level."

Arthur C. Guyton,
The Textbook of Medical Physiology, Fifth Edition

Oxygen is the most basic requirement for human life and if you go without it for five minutes you will die, yet most of us pay little attention to our breathing unless we are having respiratory problems. As infants we naturally breathe all the way to our diaphragm, but at some point in our development we began to breathe from our lungs and don't get the oxygen our bodies require. Breathing from our diaphragm links us to our higher brain and the place where the Inner Physician resides.

We have been breathing our whole lives, but very few people have been breathing correctly. Our breathing is on autopilot. One drawback to being on autopilot is we are not aware we are breathing improperly which leads to developing and carrying bad breathing habits throughout life. An astonishing number of physical ailments and diseases are rooted in poor breathing and oxygen deficits, which causes or worsens chronic maladies such as asthma, allergies, anxiety, fatigue, depression, headaches, heart conditions, high blood pressure, sleep loss, obesity, harmful stress, poor mental clarity plus hundreds of other lesser known but equally harmful conditions. It has been said that we inhale our first breath of life, we exhale our last breath of life, and every breath in between counts. Be grateful for every breath you take!

Chest breathing isn't efficient because it doesn't reach the greatest amount of blood flow which occurs in the lower lobes of the lungs. Rapid, shallow, chest breathing results in less oxygen transfer to the blood and poor delivery of nutrients to the tissues. In order to get the full effect of the breath it must be drawn in from the belly, expanding the abdomen in smooth and rhythmic movements. The purpose of breathing this deeply is to get your lungs into shape so that when you breathe normally it will be deeper and you will use more of your lungs. When breathing correctly you become more energetic and feel more alive.

The oxygen levels on the earth are actually decreasing because of the burning of fossil fuels, which consumes oxygen, and deforestation, which reduces oxygen. Now more than ever it is important to be breathing to our capacity. Even symptoms that are not caused by incorrect breathing can be eased and improved by conscious breathing practices. Did you know that breathing occurs 20,000 times each day and it happens automatically without having to think about it? It is hard to believe that one of the secrets to better health is breathing, something you are doing right now without thinking about it.

Thousands of years ago, Eastern yogis and Chinese sages developed powerful systems of breath control that they used for healing and attaining enlightenment. Many cultures believe that the process of breathing is the essence of being and breathing techniques can be found in shamanic traditions, yogic practices and healing practices around the world. Every major spiritual discipline uses a form of breath awareness as part of its practice and these ancient teachings are powerful because they tap into the spiritual life force. Using the breath as a transformational tool has a long and rich history. Many cultures use breathing techniques as a way to create and direct energy, to develop focus, and to cleanse the body of many of the toxins produced by everyday living.

There are mysterious powers associated with the breath that remain mostly unheard of in western civilization. Ancient practitioners of qigong, Chi Kung, Tai Chi and other forms of martial arts have known for a long time that disciplined intentional breathing affected physical and emotional well-being. Buddha is the most famous Eastern master who became enlightened by meditating on his breathing.

In yoga, the breath is known as prana, a universal energy that can be used to find a balance between the body-mind-spirit. It creates currents of energy in the body that control many of the unconscious functions which allow the maintenance of the physical body. It regulates the circulation of blood, digests food, affects moods and levels of stress, and these are only a few of the obvious things that are affected by the breath. Breathing practices are finding new life as people discover their potential for healing and creating balance in the body.

Rebirthing is another powerful use of the breath, which contributes more specifically to the healing of the emotional body. This method enables a person to release repressed emotional traumas locked in the cells so that they don't continue to influence the unconscious level of awareness. Rebirthing is a form of conscious breathing that is very effective at bringing awareness to life experiences that have been hidden from us and how they impact our lives. The breathing experience is guided by a Rebirthing practitioner. I have had numerous rebirthing sessions that gave me great insights and uncovered cellular trauma from this life and past lives that I wouldn't have gotten any other way.

Internationally known master of breath Andy Caponigro teaches a gentle system of breathing techniques called The Miracle of Breath, which accesses the pranic life force to assist in shifting mental and physical illness. One of the virtues of The Miracle of the Breath is that one can learn the basic meditation technique to defuse everyday stress levels. This can be taken to a higher level where you learn how to master fear and control pain. With daily practice, these techniques can unquestionably help the body heal.

Many sports psychologists teach the manipulation of breathing as a way to relax, to improve concentration, to engage the performance mindset, and to gain self-control. They use it as a way to visualize and implant success in the minds of the athlete before a big game. Some researchers believe that proper breathing and breathing practices can eliminate all stress-induced neurological disorders and the need for anti-depressant drugs, sedatives or even mild painkillers. It is as though breathing has become the new natural wonder drug in some circles. Think of the money that could be saved on pharmaceuticals using the breath to heal.

There has been a resurgence of interest in ancient practices that utilize breath to explore and empower the inner self. Breathing is an excellent tool for facilitating positive change because it is the most efficient way to communicate with all the systems of the body and it is maintained by the Inner Physician. It is the only bodily function that we do both voluntarily and involuntarily. Breathing exercises can act as a bridge into the functions of the body that generally aren't under our conscious control. We can consciously use breathing to influence the sympathetic nervous system that regulates blood pressure, heart rate, circulation, digestion and many other bodily functions. This is why my spontaneous breath work was so effective at shutting down my elimination system when I had the strangulated bowel. Imagine how this simple tool could help you on your journey back to wellness!

I came upon the miracle of breath quite by accident and it saved my life, or at least it seemed like it was an accident. I believe that I was inspired to breathe in such a way by something higher and the controlled breathing turned my elimination systems off. I started the breathing technique I used during labor because I knew it might help with pain reduction. I am grateful that it did so much more.

Intentional breathing is a powerful tool that brings us into the present and away from the thinking mind, which keeps us hooked to our story of the past and the future. When we are in the midst of pain our thinking mind creates a story of being stuck in the pain for the rest of our lives and that is all we can think about. As long as we stay with that story we will continue to feel our pain. If we begin to pay attention to our breathing, one breath at a time, it brings us into the present moment and into the space where we can heal ourselves in an instant. The present moment is where our Inner Physician lives and we can access that intelligence through our breath.

Scientists have known for a long time that there is a strong connection between respiration and the mental states. I learned by accident, in the midst of a life- threatening disorder, how important breath can be. When I engaged intentional breathing, change happened. Using mindful intentional breathing techniques, individuals have learned to control their heartbeats, blood flow, blood pressure, immune system, mental conditions and even pain.

Let's look at the word inspiration for a minute because the meanings are quite interesting with regard to the breath. It is interesting that in most languages, the word for breath is the same as the word for spirit. The word inspiration comes from the word spirit. Breath is spirit, which is the life force and the significant carrier of energy in the human system.

If you look up the definition of the word inspiration you will find this: 1) The act of inspiring or breathing in; breath; the drawing of air or other gases into the lungs, accomplished in mammals by elevation of the chest walls and flattening of the diaphragm; the opposite of expiration. 2) The act or power of exercising an elevating or stimulating influence upon the intellect or emotions; the result of such influence which quickens or stimulates; as, the inspiration of occasion, of art, etc.; arousal of the mind to special unusual activity or creativity. 3) A supernatural divine influence on the prophets, apostles, or sacred writers, by which they were qualified to communicate moral or religious truth with authority; a supernatural influence which qualifies men to receive and communicate divine truth; also, the truth communicated. (theology) A special influence of a divinity on the minds of human beings; "They believe that the books of Scripture were written under divine guidance." 4) A product of your creative thinking and work; "He had little respect for the inspirations of other artists"; "After years of work his brainchild was a tangible reality." 5) A sudden intuition as part of solving a problem.

As you can see the act of inspiration is one that influences the body, mind and spirit. Breath is the spirit, nourishing us on the inhale and cleansing us on the exhale.

Breath is divinely inspired and it is a function taken care of by the Inner Physician. If you are experiencing pain or discomfort right now, close your eyes and begin to breathe.

On the inbreath imagine spirit nourishing you as the breath fills your body. On the outbreath imagine that the pain and discomfort is being cleansed away. Take a few minutes to do this so you can be more present with this writing.

AWAKENING YOUR INNER PHYSICIAN

Here are some breathing techniques you might want to try for yourself to see if this is something that will work for you:

Relaxing Sigh:

The first technique is the relaxing sigh. It is simple and you can do it any time of the day. Sighing and yawning during the day are signs that you are not getting enough oxygen. A conscious sighing practice can be a great stress release.

1. Sit or stand up straight so your spine is erect.

2. Sigh deeply, letting out a sound of deep relief as the air rushes out of   your lungs.

3. Let new air come in naturally.

4. Repeat this procedure eight to twelve times whenever you feel the need for it, and experience the feeling of relaxation. If you are feeling tense or going into a stressful situation, do this exercise.

Abdominal Breathing Technique:

Try doing this breathing exercise twice a day or whenever you find your mind dwelling on upsetting thoughts or when you are experiencing pain. Most of us do not get air all the way into our abdomen each time we breathe so over time this exercise will improve your overall health and wellness.

1. Place one hand on your chest and the other on your abdomen. When you take a deep breath in, the hand on the abdomen should rise higher than the one on the chest. This insures that the diaphragm is pulling air into the bases of the lungs.

2. After exhaling through the mouth, take a slow deep breath in through your nose imagining that you are sucking in all the air in the room and hold it for a count of 7.

3. Slowly exhale through your mouth for a count of 8. As all the air is released with relaxation, gently contract your abdominal muscles to release all of the air from the lungs. We deepen respiration not by inhaling more air but through completely exhaling it. Exhaling in this way takes practice.

4. Repeat the cycle four more times for a total of 5 deep breaths and try to breathe at a rate of one breath every 10 seconds (or 6 breaths per minute). At this rate our heart rate variability increases which has a positive effect on cardiac health.

Deep Breathing:

This technique is easy yet takes concentration in the beginning to keep doing it. You may feel lightheaded when you first start to practice it. After you get used to deep breathing, it then becomes second nature again. The basic steps to deep breathing are:

1. Take a deep breath through the nose, making sure your stomach expands as you breathe in.

2. Hold the breath in for the count of 5.

3. Release your breath out through your mouth emptying your lungs the best you can.

4. Count to 5 and begin a deep breath in again.

5. Repeat this for about 10 breaths every day until that becomes normal.

The great thing about breathing exercises is they are very portable. You can take them wherever you go and use them when you need them. Find a breathing technique that works for you and add it to your daily routine.

CHAPTER FOUR

There Are No Accidents

"Accidents, try to change them, it's impossible. The accidental reveals man."

Pablo Picasso

We have all heard the expression "there are no accidents," which implies that everything that happens to us is meant to be. We create our lives and draw to us experiences that give us lessons that we need to learn. There are no accidents, only opportunities to help us grow and learn. It is up to us to choose how we are going to respond to our experiences and it is our response that carries us in the direction we end up going. It is hard to believe that I have attracted four major car accidents. Even though it is said that there are not accidents, each one of them sure felt like one at the time, and yet each one supplied me with lessons and growth.

The first accident happened in 1968, three months after my brother's accidental death by drowning in a river north of our home. I was 17 and Patrick was 18 the year he died. My grieving was deep because he was the one sibling that I felt I had a connection with. The night before he died he made a strong statement about how much he cared about me, by sticking up for me when I was being harassed by someone. Before that I wasn't really sure he cared.

I somehow held myself responsible for his death because I woke him up so he could go to the river with friends where he ended up drowning, and I held onto that belief for many years. Maybe it gave me a sense of control over a situation that made no sense to me because he was brilliant and had a promising future ahead of him. For three months I sat on our porch swing every day and didn't leave or talk with any of my friends. One day I finally agreed to go out with a friend for a few hours. Not far from my home we ended up in an accident, sandwiched between two other cars. They took us both to the hospital to check for injuries. I had pain in my neck so they put me in a neck brace and said I could go home. I had to call my still traumatized parents and tell them I was in the hospital due to an accident and needed a ride home. As a result of the accident I had whiplash injuries which I recovered from quickly because I was young and resilient. It did create a sort of an Achilles heel that set my body up for future injuries.

The first accident I was involved in as an adult happened ten years later in 1978.

I was driving on a city street at rush hour when a woman in the other lane going the opposite direction came into my lane and hit my car head on. In the heavy rush hour traffic, my car bounced off her car and slammed into the back of a car that was parked at the side of the road. As the accident was occurring I locked my arms in place on the steering wheel taking both impacts into my arms, which injured my neck, shoulders and back. My body went through two impacts before the car came to rest. If you were to see photos of my car you would be surprised that I survived because both cars were totaled. The front end of my car was pushed straight up in the air, so you couldn't see the windshield. Once again I was taken to the hospital by ambulance and sent home in a neck brace.

Because of the long-term nature of my injuries I became involved in a personal injury lawsuit. It stretched out over three years as I went to numerous doctors who tried to prove that I was lying because I wanted money. They have an actual psychological diagnosis for this, called malingering. Malingering is a medical and psychological term that refers to an individual fabricating or exaggerating the symptoms of mental or physical disorders for a variety of motives, including getting financial compensation often tied to fraud, avoiding work, obtaining drugs, getting lighter criminal sentences, trying to get out of going to school, or simply to attract attention or sympathy. The truth was I wanted to heal and be out of pain and no amount of money could replace that! It was a humiliating experience to have people trying to prove I was either crazy or faking it when in fact I was experiencing real pain. Someone had come to this conclusion because I had drawings of the areas of my body where I had pain. As a visual person it was easier for me to describe the pain using a drawing to give my doctor a clear picture of my pain so they could figure out what was wrong and make it better. To the psychiatrists who were assessing me this was a true sign that I was faking my symptoms. In the end, the settlement I received could not make up for the humiliation and suffering I experienced in the process. I swore I would never get involved in another lawsuit if I had another car accident, no matter how bad I was injured, because it was such a horrific experience.

When I gave birth to my daughter two years later I had so much pain in my back, a result of my injuries, that I had to close my graphic arts business, which I had spent two years building. For two years following the accident I could not draw or paint because there was so much pain in my shoulder, arm and hand. I couldn't hold a pen or pencil for more than a couple of minutes before my hand cramped up. My problem was exacerbated by lifting my new baby and carrying her from place to place. I stopped painting because it wasn't worth the time it took to recover afterward. This was devastating and I couldn't help but think it might be permanent and I would have to give up my career as an artist, which was a dream I had since I was a child. Chronic pain is difficult to live with and it is hard to stay positive when all you can think about is the pain that you feel every day. It is easy to become discouraged, angry and crabby, feelings I had every day. I understand first-hand what people who are in chronic pain go through every day and how it impacts the quality of life.

After several years of chronic arm and shoulder pain I experienced another miracle. One cold winter day I was leaving to go shopping. I put my three-year-old daughter Carrie into her car seat and walked back to the garage to close the door not realizing that the middle finger on my right hand was stuck in between one of the slats. Because the door was heavy it went all the way down to the ground before I could pull it back up. When I raised the door and pulled my finger out it was crushed and the back of it had split open. Fortunately I couldn't feel the pain because it froze immediately from the cold, thank God. I went to the emergency room where the doctor pushed a hot paper clip through my nail to relieve the pressure from blood buildup. I was surprised at the barbaric instrument which he told me was the best thing they had found for doing the job. My fractured finger was put in a splint. Here is where the miracle comes in. After six weeks, my finger was healed and the pain syndrome that had been trapped in my shoulder for five years was gone! I could use my hand and my shoulder was pain free!

I was elated because after five years of wishing the pain would go away, a freak accident had taken it away immediately. If I knew that would happen I might have found a way to crush my finger a long time ago. I say that partly in jest and partly in truth because five years is a long time to have chronic pain and if it was this simple I wish I had known. I think it is possible that when my finger was smashed the pressure hit an acupressure point that ran up my arm and into my shoulder and that is what released the condition.

I wish I had savored every minute of my pain-free life because two years later I was involved in another serious car accident. When you feel good there is a tendency to take it for granted but when you are in pain you can't get it off your mind. I was so used to feeling good that I forgot how I had felt when I was in pain. In retrospect I should have been grateful every day! Why isn't gratitude a built-in response like suffering is?

When the third accident occurred I was on a major freeway in St. Paul, returning from dinner at my boyfriend's house. I had just bought a new house after searching for a year and was getting my life back together after my divorce. I was so happy and excited for my new beginning. The sun was just setting when I started the drive home and I was only a mile away from home when I got an intuitive thought that I should exit the freeway. I wrestled with this because I wasn't at my exit so it didn't make any sense to get off. As I fought with myself about getting off the freeway the truck in front of me quickly pulled out and before I could do anything my car was slamming into the back of another car that was parked in the middle of the freeway with its lights turned off. Yes, I said parked. In the time it took for me to hit this car, which was a matter of seconds, my life flashed before me in slow motion. I remember thinking, "Damn, just when things start going well, I am going to die!"

My car hit the parked car and bounced backward before I could stop it and as it did my body went forward and hit the steering wheel and my head flew back and hit the headrest, while my knee slammed into some part of the door. As my car flew backward the other car burst into flames because it was old and the gas tank was in the back.

When I came to a stop all I could think of was getting out of the car before it blew up. I had seen too many car chase movies where that had happened. Without thinking, I jumped from my car and started crawling across the freeway to get to the side. I had to crawl because of the pain I was in. As I got past the back of my car and into the lane next to me at least a dozen cars came to a screeching halt before hitting me. There were definitely angels watching over me.

I had pain in my chest and was afraid something had happened to my heart and I couldn't hold my head up because my neck was so weak. On the way to the hospital the two paramedics who were tending to me were laughing because they said the man parked his car in the middle of the freeway because he wanted to retrieve a piece of carpet from the road. I don't know if they were kidding or not but they described this man pulling out a vacuum from his trunk and vacuuming the carpet in the middle of the freeway. To be honest I would have much rather hit a piece of carpet because hitting a parked car going 50 miles an hour is like hitting a brick wall. My boyfriend picked me up from the hospital and I left in a neck brace with another severe case of whiplash, back, shoulder and arm injuries and a badly bruised knee.

You might remember that I said I would never get involved in another lawsuit again because of the humiliation and emotional pain it caused, yet once again I found myself in that arena. The man who parked his car on the freeway decided to sue me for rear-ending him so I had to hire an attorney to represent me in this bizarre case. Of all of the 1000's of attorneys he could have picked he hired the one who represented me in my previous lawsuit. This is more mind boggling because this man lives in Wisconsin and my former attorney lives in Minnesota. I called the lawyer and told him who I was and informed him that he had a client who was suing me; when he found out who it was he dropped the case due to conflict of interest. In the end the man contacted several attorneys who wouldn't take the case after they found out the circumstances, so there I was in a lawsuit, suing him! In case you are wondering, they settled out of court and I won because no one could believe that someone would stop in the middle of the freeway to pick up carpet at rush hour.

Once again the money could not make up for the pain and suffering I was feeling from another pain complex in my shoulder, arm and hand. The pain I experienced on a daily basis was like someone pinching me in the shoulder so hard that I wanted to scream. I had pain most of the time when I was awake and at night it was hard to sleep because my hands went numb and my shoulder would pop out of place. Now my doctor was telling me that I would never heal and would have to learn to live with it. One of my doctors gave me a 40% permanent disability in my right arm and told me it would get worse over time and as I aged I would eventually have frozen shoulder. Frozen shoulder is characterized by pain and loss of motion or stiffness in the shoulder and results in an inability to lift your arm. I remember thinking to myself, at the time, "No! I am not going to accept that I have to live with a permanent injury in my arm and hand, I am an artist!" Talk about having bad "car-ma"! Sorry, I couldn't resist.

In retrospect when I wonder why I would call these accidents to me I realize my unconscious programming was about not being worthy or deserving of good things. When good things began to happen my programming would create a new drama to prove that I was right about not being deserving. Because of the unconscious programming this would create something that would take away all the happiness I was feeling as I created a new life for myself.

I lived with this pain for another four years. It was worse in the winter when it was cold and I would have the pinching pain all the time. One day I decided that I was going to find a way to make it go away again. I knew by this time that I had pretty good healing ability and if I could do it once I could do it again. No I didn't go out and find a garage door to slam my hand in; I didn't have the guts to do that. What came to me seemed kind of ridiculous at the time but I did it anyway. I took a week of vacation from work, so I wouldn't have to use my arm and could focus all of my time on getting better. Every day I immobilized my arm for several hours and lay in front of my stereo playing music to my arm and shoulder. I played classical, rock, jazz, new age and world music to my damaged arm, thinking healing thoughts. Each day I repeated the process and by the end of the week the pain had cleared. This is the kind of guidance that can only come from the Inner Physician. It seems strange but I knew it was important for me to follow it. This happened in 1989. I am still pain free and today I rarely have a flare-up unless I overdo using my arm.

I had given my body what it needed so it could release and repair itself by playing music to it and honoring its need to be still and quiet. Dr. Christiane Northrup says, "The more you move toward what makes you feel good, and move away from those things which bring you distress and pain, the healthier you will be." My body wanted music for its healing and listening to music helped me feel good. I was beginning to see that each time I listened to the requests from my Inner Physician and experienced success, my resolve strengthened and trust in the wisdom of my body grew. Through the process I developed trust in my body and knew it could find its own balance and equilibrium if I let it.

Doctors don't realize when they tell patients that they are not going to get better, or that they have a fatal disease, they are cementing that reality in place so it is sure to come true. We are taught to believe everything the doctor says, as if it is gospel, and not to question it so when they tell us we have a permanent condition or a terminal disease we believe what they say. Once we own a diagnosis we are on our way to a self-fulfilling prophecy. Now we are saying to ourselves and everyone who asks, "I have cancer" or "I have a heart condition," And so we do. Fortunately for me I am too stubborn to listen, especially when someone tells me there is nothing I can do. I don't take no for an answer very well.

I listened to my Inner Physician, who had an understanding about what my body needed and I was healed!

You won't believe this but just as I was finishing this book I had car accident number four. I was on a busy freeway in the Twin Cities, going about 50 miles per hour when a moving van three cars ahead of me came to a dead stop. The two cars ahead of me swerved to the right and I swerved to the left and caught the left bumper of the woman in front of me. Though we were all going 55 miles per hour, no one lost control and now the woman I hit was behind me as we drove off the nearest exit ramp to exchange information. It is amazing that this accident wasn't worse giving the speed everyone was going.

I noticed pain in my neck immediately. After a consult with a chiropractor I learned that my symptoms – headache, dizziness, and memory problems – were consistent with a concussion. I thought a concussion was caused by hitting your head but it can also come from a neck traction injury such as whiplash. I began working with a chiropractor who specializes in working with people who have concussions and she told me that this work can clear up both old and new concussions.

As I was getting up from my first treatment, the room started spinning and I felt like I was going to pass out. It was so bad that the doctor had to drive me home. The interesting thing was, the feeling I had was the same feeling I had when I fell from a wall and broke my wrist four years earlier. At the time the focus was on my wrist and my knees and no one thought to check out my head. I believe that I had a concussion back then and I have been having memory issues ever since, and this accident shined the light on it so I could have the treatment to clear it up. Without this accident I would not have been aware that I had a problem so this seems like another miracle to me.

I also got an interesting insight from the accident that I needed to discover. There were several things happening in the days following the accident that caused a lot of stress on me and got me into an old pattern of ruminating. I decided to journal and ask my guide for insight and this is what I got.

"The car is a powerful metaphor for how much control/power you have. You never lost control of the car, it was masterful. You can have the same mastery over your thoughts. Get back on track energetically. Come back into balance. Right yourself as masterfully as you righted your car. If you can do that with a car going 50 miles an hour you can do the same thing with your thoughts. This is a metaphor for how you let things throw you off and you are learning quick recovery. These are just blips on the radar and you need to see them as such. Someone says something you don't like, it is just a blip! Things don't go the way you planned, just a blip! Keep going. No one can throw you off course except you! No one! Don't let the illusion stand in the way of your dreams, happiness and joy."

Our thoughts can be just as powerful on the road to creating our desires as a car can on the road to our destination. They can cause disaster if we let them or they can get us where we want to go.

We are socialized to give our power away to people in authority. For patients who do not question their doctor the option to return to wellness is taken away by the doctor's proclamation. What if every doctor proclaimed that there was hope and every patient hung on their every word so hope became resolve and resolve opened up the space for well-being to return? I could not allow myself to believe I wouldn't get better because it meant giving up my art career and living in pain for the rest of my life and I wasn't interested in that. If I had believed what my doctor said about my injury who knows where I would be right now? Don't get me wrong, I am not saying we shouldn't believe our doctors, I just have an issue with them telling us things that they don't know are true for sure. No one can predict how each unique body/mind/spirit is going to react to disharmony. All this does is implant a suggestion that could come true because we begin to believe it.

Our minds are suggestible and our consciousness doesn't know fact from fiction.

In co-creation we get what we ask for even if it isn't conscious. In the words of Abraham-Hicks, one of my favorite wise beings, "There is no condition that you cannot modify into something more, any more than there is any painting that you can paint and not like and just paint over it again. There are many limiting thoughts in the human environment that make it feel like it is not so, as you have these incurable illnesses, or these unchangeable conditions. But we say they are only 'unchangeable' because you believe that they are." Anything is possible in the realm of health and wellness and the wisdom of the Inner Physician and there is no such thing as false hope. Hope is hope and positive thoughts promote wellness.

Let's explore how to use sound in healing and share ideas how to use it for yourself.

CREATIVE TECHNIQUE
FOR WELLNESS

Sound Health & Wellness

"The body is held together by sound – the presence of disease indicates that some sounds have gone out of tune."

Dr. Deepak Chopra

Sound, the original creational tone, has been recognized as a healing force for thousands of years by ancient civilizations. Many of those ancient techniques have been lost over time with Westerners thinking shamanism was spiritual quackery or primitive. Traditional cultures still surviving today understand the remarkable healing power that lies in sound. Shamans around the world have used sound in healing rituals, using the voice, drums and rattles. The sound of the drum connects with the heartbeat of the earth and our own heartbeat and when we hear it we become entrained. I have been fortunate enough to be trained as a Kultrun carrier in the Mapuche tradition by my friend and medicine woman Luzclara in Chile. We work with a drum that is only for women. It is made like a bowl, covered with animal skin and filled with sacred objects. It is only used in healing sound ceremonies.

The idea of using sound for healing is experiencing a recent revival because people are realizing how effective it is. I love the idea of using sound for wellness because sound knows exactly where to go to find blockages and disharmony in the body, release them with ease and bring the body back to balance. Sound is vibration and we resonate with certain sounds according to our own vibration. Sound vibration directly aligns all of our energy fields. Like Deepak Chopra says, the body is held together by sound. This is why using sound created a healing environment for my arm, hand and shoulder. I had picked a vibration that made it feel good and it was able to relax and heal.

Sound is an extremely powerful tool for wellness, personal growth, and spiritual transformation. For centuries, it has been used successfully to induce states of physical, mental, and emotional relaxation. It allows a person to enter into personal and sacred space where they can journey deep into their inner resources to retrieve information, energy, renewed vitality, balance, clarity, inspiration, relaxation, creativity, free expression, and transformation.

We begin to explore sound at the moment of birth. When babies begin to communicate they do so using cooing or babbling sounds. No matter what the native language of the parents, babies all over the world utter a similar sound: mmmm, mum, mu, ma, as they grope their way toward speech. Before there was language man was communicating with sound, through the voice and using instruments.

I find it interesting that Webster defines "healing" as "to make sound." It can also be interpreted as "to become sound." Our body is a self-healing instrument with a genetic blueprint for health, orchestrated by the Inner Physician and every organ, bone and cell has its own resonant frequency or tone. We become ill when we lose the sacred balance with our true essence and fall out of harmony with the program within our DNA. Sounds vibrate us into a state of resonance with our natural rhythm and state of harmony and health.

Every cell in our body is a sound resonator and lives in a rhythmic pattern. The various systems and organs in our body respond to sound vibrations as do our mental, emotional, and spiritual states of consciousness.

All things in nature vibrate to sound, light and color and so does everything in our environment. Our senses are bombarded and impacted by sound all the time whether we are aware of the sound or not. Some sounds create discomfort and other sounds cause resonant harmony. Some sounds can be calming and soothing and others can be disruptive and nerve wracking. A loud banging sound can make you jump in fear and a kitten purring can make you melt. I find fireworks for example disruptive to my vibration where many people just love them, though it is hard to imagine they might be soothing to anyone.

The combination of our own vibration and that of music is why some of us like Jazz where others might like Opera, or Country and Western. We resonate with what feels good to our ears. Some music makes us anxious and some has a calming effect. Everything is in a state of vibration and all vibration is perceived as sound on subtle and not so subtle levels.

I have always had very good hearing and am sensitive to sound. I am one of those who can wake up if a pin drops in the room where I am sleeping. When my daughter, Carrie, was a teenager we had an ongoing discussion every time she was in the car with me. She wanted to listen to "her music" which was not music to my ears. I told her I felt that it made me agitated and cranky when I drove. One day I wasn't aware that she had changed the channel on the car radio until I began to swear at drivers and get angry at the simplest thing. I am usually a very calm driver. When I realized it was the music she had turned on I changed the channel and my mood changed almost immediately. Carrie stopped testing my theory after that.

A few years ago she was driving my car and changed the channel. When I got into the car the next day and began driving I wasn't conscious of my speed and when I got pulled over by a cop for speeding I realized it was because of the music on the radio. When he approached my car to ask for my license I shared my theory with him. He looked at me like I was crazy and took my license back to his car. When he returned he told me he wouldn't give me a speeding ticket but a driving without seatbelts ticket which wouldn't impact my record. Of course I was wearing a seat belt at the time. I don't know if he believed my theory or just felt sorry for a crazy woman, but I think he will ponder the impact of sound.

Inner harmony is disrupted by stress, trauma, and negative emotional and mental patterns which we can bring it back into balance using sound and frequency. If we know the frequency of something we can change it through sound and by playing the missing frequencies can return the system to wholeness, health and harmony. The body is like an orchestra receiving and producing a symphony of sounds, chemicals, electrical charges, colors, and images. When we are in good health, the instruments in our orchestra perform fluidly and in tune. When we are sick or ailing, one or more instrument is out of tune.

Sound can produce order out of randomness, by causing an energy system to synchronize with itself, producing standing waves. It is possible to experience powerful physical healing by harmonizing the emotional body. When the emotional, spiritual and mental bodies are brought into alignment through sound, health can occur. When we release the blockages using sound we can come back into harmony and balance.

Sound healing is the therapeutic application of sound frequencies to the body and mind of a person with the intention of bringing them into a state of harmony and health. It is not the same as music therapy though that also uses sound. Sound healing is the practice of using sound to discover and correct imbalances in the body. Sound healing works on the belief that the human body is energy that is held together by sound, like Chopra stated. Disease indicates that some sound has gone out of tune.

There are many different instruments used in sound healing including crystal and Tibetan bowls and tuning forks, rattles and drums but the most powerful instrument is the voice.

The voice is the most powerful and potent vehicle to bring about alignment. The sound of the voice speaks to the soul. The sound of your own voice is your most powerful medicine.

One of my teachers, Jonathan Goldman, Director of the Sound Healers Association and author of Healing Sounds: The Power of Harmonics, says, "...of all the sound making devices and instruments found on this planet, the human voice is believed by many to have the most healing qualities." I spent nine days in Colorado at Jonathan Goldman's Sound Healing Intensive. We were immersed in the high vibration of sound for nine days. I learned very quickly that at that level of vibration there is no place to hide, especially from yourself. Sound has a way of bringing to consciousness things that need to be seen and things that are out of balance. As the Healing Sound Intensive progressed I discovered the truth in what Jonathan said about the voice. Our voices have the capacity to create many different sounds.

Toning, which is defined as "to make sound with an elongated vowel for an extended period," requires no special instruments other than your voice. It is an ancient method of healing used to restore your harmonic patterns. We can learn to use our voice and resonate different areas of our body and bring them into balance. Toning releases tension in specific areas, induces relaxation, energy, and promotes deep breathing and prolonged exhalation. Energetically, it balances the body's subtle energies and powerfully draws the awareness deep within.

Toning with other people creates a feeling of unity. It also helps us to release stress and repressed emotions. Regular toning and humming help to reenergize the body and restore health to the mind, body and spirit. Toning has an effect on the body which has been found to boost the immune system and release endorphins. Jonathan Goldman offers the simple formula, "Frequency plus Intention equals Healing." If we can find a pure sound frequency coupled with a pure intention then healing will occur. When our body receives a pure tone our muscles will relax and tension will be released. If we add intention to sound as we tone the results are powerful.

At the Sound Healing Intensive we participated in a day of toning, which was about 10-11 hours long. We took turns toning for an hour at a time rotating as groups and when we were not toning, we were in silence. This was a powerful experience as I watched myself spin around in thoughts and judgment that surprised me. I was able to transform the thoughts using sound and move to a place of compassion for everyone in the group who had made a commitment to hold this sacred space for the day so that we all could benefit. It was a difficult process shifting from judgment when I was all alone with my thoughts! The sound helped me transform.

When I was a young girl, from about 4 years old to 8, I used to sit on the couch at home and sing the sound "AH." I had a special place on the mohair couch in my parents' living room and no one else could sit in my "bouncing spot." Four or five times a day I would sit in this spot and rock back and forth singing "AH, AH, AH." Everyone in the family honored this space for me though I am sure they all thought I was a bit strange. If someone was sitting in "my spot" and I came in they got up and left, on some level knowing this was important for me. The sound of "AH" brought me comfort. We moved when I was 8 and the couch was discarded and my singing stopped. I know that my heart missed the song.

Many years later I learned that what I was singing was the heart chant. I made this discovery twenty years ago during my studies with a Native American teacher who taught us to chant a vowel sound for each of the chakras. The sound of the heart was "AH" and it would awake love within. As I chanted the "AH" sound as an adult my heart began to remember again. Somehow as a young girl I remembered the comfort of love within my own heart as it rose on the sound of "AH" and how I intuitively knew how to activate it. At the Healing Sound Intensive with Jonathan Goldman I learned about the power of the sound of "AH" to open and expand the heart chakra. The sound of "AH" is one of the sounds that brings about the response of love. It vibrates the heart center when you sound it and awakens loving feelings. It is the sound that awakens compassion.

The "AH" sound is a sacred seed syllable. The "AH" is a universal, non- denominational heart sound that when projected with focused energy is extremely powerful and effective. It is non-denominational because as a vowel sound, everyone accepts it as a mantra. In most mystical traditions around the world the sound of "AH" is the sound equated with the heart chakra. To activate healing and a feeling of love sing your heart the love song of "AH."

AWAKENING YOUR INNER PHYSICIAN

Here is a simple way Jonathan Goldman teaches to experience the sound of "AH." "To do this, simply sound the "AH," feeling the energy of peace and compassion as the sound resonates in your heart center. While making this "AH," visualize a beam of pink and gold energy going initially from you and spreading throughout the planet. As you make this sound, and do this visualization, feel the energy of peace and compassion within and outside of yourself. This feeling of peace while you make the sound is essential to the effectiveness of projecting the "AH."

Here is another exercise using the "AH" sound that is extremely beneficial for developing compassion within self and then generating it to others. Start with yourself first and begin to tone the "AH" sound while feeling the energy of compassion and peace within. Once you have been able to achieve this feeling, visualize a person with whom you have neutral energy and send this energy to them while making this sound. Finally, make the "AH" sound while sending the energy of peace and compassion to someone with whom you've had some difficulty. It is this last part of the exercise that provides the greatest opportunity for spiritual growth. It is easy to send love and peace to someone you already love, or, with the second part of the exercise, someone you don't have any real feelings about. It can be a real challenge to send compassion to someone you don't love and whom you may consider to be an enemy. Yet, herein lies the most extraordinary evolutionary activation that can occur on both a personal and planetary level. If we can learn to do this, we will greatly assist the ascension of the Earth.

Try this yourself and experience the comfort of the sound of the heart. You might also try toning "AH" while focusing on your illness. Visualize that part of you that is feeling disease as you fill it with love, peace and compassion. Pay attention and notice if there is anything that shifts in the process.

CHAPTER FIVE

Awaken the Goddess

"God may be in the details, but the Goddess is in the questions. Once we begin to ask them, there's no turning back."

Gloria Steinem

Indigenous forms of healing and spirituality have always fascinated me. I love the natural way that Indigenous people go about bringing back health and have great respect for shamans. In 1996 I was involved in a year-long study group on shamanism which focused on using the Peruvian Medicine Wheel. In one of the directions on the medicine wheel we were required to explore our fears. This process manifested in me on a physical level with a severe sore throat and anxiety attacks that came from a feeling my throat was closing off. The sore throat went on for months and at one point I was afraid I might have throat cancer, but I was afraid to go to the doctor and find out. My vivid imagination didn't serve me in this situation because I tended to hitch my wagon to a negative story. This was before I knew about the law of attraction. Many times I would feel as though my throat were closing off and as I struggled to breathe I would go into an anxiety attack which someone would have to talk me out of.

Over the six months I had the symptoms I became aware of a deep fear of having something wrong and that I might die. The fear made sense given what I had experienced in the past but I didn't want it to be what drove my life, so I decided to do an in-depth exploration to uncover and release it for good. I also knew that if I could get to the root and shift the issue, I would get better physically.

The throat chakra, which is the energy center at the throat, is connected with communication and it is very common for women to have blocks in this area. The reason for this is deep and ancient, and comes from past lives of oppression and death for speaking out as a woman. Even in current times it hasn't been that long since women were given the right to vote and we are just beginning to take back our power. One of the important tasks we have as women is to birth our voice. This is exactly what I was doing and the birthing process can be quite painful.

One day I was having so much trouble swallowing that the art therapist in me told me to draw what I was feeling. I was at my art studio and I said to myself, "You are an art therapist, draw what you are feeling for God's sake!" What occurred was a very rapid emergence of a woman with rainbow hair, doves flying from her head, a star at her throat and a tree growing from her torso.

Through my drawing of this image I was able to transform the scar left from my intestinal surgery into a tree of life. My scar is really a symbol of life for me so the tree of life seemed perfect. I also gave wings to my voice by painting doves coming from my throat. It was an extremely empowering image for me.

As I looked at the image it occurred to me that this was the Goddess and She wanted to emerge and be heard. I also knew that it was only the first of many images to come. For the next two months images flowed through me in rapid succession. I found myself overwhelmed by images of the

Goddess which arrived fully pictured and intensely energized. They came when I was driving, working, sleeping and eating, so many images that I wasn't able to capture them all in paint. As I type these words I feel a tickling sensation in my throat and I have to cough. I know that writing this book is as important as creating the Goddess images. I have resisted writing this book because I felt that it was too complicated to capture all of the things I had gone through and put them into some kind of order. I wasn't sure I wanted to be so vulnerable by sharing my experiences and I also wondered if it really mattered. I was afraid of what people might think about all of these bizarre things that have happened to me and the weird things I have done to heal. Now I am finding the writing is just flowing through my fingertips, just as the images of the Goddess did, as though I am only a scribe taking dictation. The book wants to be written and I am the only thing in the way. Now it is more important to get the stories out than to worry about what people will think of me. I feel like if one word, one sentence or a paragraph that I have written here has an impact on someone's healing process I will have accomplished what I intended to do by writing this book and sharing my experiences.

The paintings of the Goddess made me realize that there was something much deeper and bigger than myself as a human involved in the process. On Mother's Day the same year that the images flooded me I had an experience with the Goddess that was like finding the mother who could give me all of the things that I wished my biological mother could give me. The experience was so real and the impact so deep that I made a decision to support and be a vehicle for the emerging feminine as part of my mission.

By the time I came to the end of the process of creating the images of the Goddess, which took two months, I had painted 44 Goddess Paintings, sometimes two or three in one day. The miraculous part of the process was that not only did my sore throat go away but I had a deeper understanding of my divine feminine nature. This series of paintings began a deep transformational journey for me that goes on even today. I learned that my images are prophetic and sometimes the messages aren't released for years after they are painted. There are times when I look at them and new information floods me.

It has been through these images and subsequent paintings that I have to come to know who I truly am as a woman, an artist, a wellness facilitator and a visionary. Each of those aspects is very important to who I am and why I am here on Earth and I had spent most of my life ignoring them or minimizing them. I remember taking the MMPI, a personality inventory, two separate times and being told that I was off the charts in my feminine energy. It was so high that it was in an area that wasn't even on the chart. The first time I took it I was sitting in a psychologist's office wearing a plaid flannel men's shirt and jeans looking more masculine than feminine. There were many years I was ashamed of being a woman because of what I had experienced both as a child and as an adult. I minimized my ability to paint, saying things to myself, such as, "It's no big deal, I am just painting." I wasn't aware that I was a visionary and a conduit for wellness. The Goddess told me differently as I painted her image.

The following year the images were published as a meditation deck called "Awaken the Goddess: An Intuitive Meditation Deck for the Emerging Feminine." I hadn't intended for this to happen, I was just painting what I felt and capturing the images that were coming through me. My son and daughter and I drove to a friend's metaphysical bookstore one day and I brought the paintings with me. The kids groaned as I pulled out the paintings because they had been with me on other occasions when I showed them to people. This time was different. When my friend Marya looked at the images she said, "I had an intuitive reading yesterday and I was told that I needed to explore the Goddess, but not the traditional images. I am supposed to find new images that resonate with me. This is just what I am looking for." After we talked a bit she agreed to help me publish them into a meditation deck that other people could use to explore the Divine Feminine too. I was so happy to have my two children watch this process because it was showing them that magical things can happen when you least expect it and when you are following your inner guidance.

Before the deck was published I learned what I had tapped into when I met the late Ron Mangravite, an esoteric teacher, mystic and expert on symbolism. He was a consultant for the movie Amityville Horrors. He was shocked to learn that I didn't have years of study about symbolism and the Goddess because he felt I had tapped into the essence of the Goddess through the images.

When we presented "Awaken the Goddess" to the public, Ron took time out of his busy schedule to fly to Minnesota from North Carolina to do a workshop on the symbolism in the images. He was going to write a companion book for the deck about the symbolism but died before that happened. As I sat in the audience listening to him talk about my paintings I was completely stunned by what he said about the wisdom of the images. After all I was just following my inner prompting and creating images from them. I didn't know that the Goddess was speaking through me.

I share his words, not to impress you, but to impress upon you what kind of miracles can happen if we listen to the inner guidance. I could have struggled for a long time with the sore throat, gone to the doctor for some kind of medication and missed an opportunity to learn something important about myself while at the same time creating a group of images that have helped many women around the world. So here are Ron's words:

"What I am here to share with you is some relatively academic knowledge which I thought was rather superficial and well known to Katelyn, but to my surprise, none of her work came out of academic studies. It just came up out of where it is supposed to come out of, which doesn't really happen much anymore. For me this presentation is a question of introducing a real live person who is doing extraordinary stuff.

This is not an opening of just some pretty exciting art, this is a public introduction to a woman who has found her inner identity in such a way that it transcends anything she is as a citizen, an inhabitant of Minneapolis, even as a woman and certainly as an artist.

I began studying exactly what is happening in the consciousness of a person who can get these phenomenal telepathic test scores, who can heal someone by touching them with their hand, who can walk into a so-called haunted house and proceed to describe with relative accuracy the past history of some of the people who lived there. Where does that come from? Rather than saying that it's a weird thing, I wanted to know the why of it. The pursuit of that converts the searcher. I became a mystic and then discovered some of the things that are going to give me great pleasure to point out how Katelyn is also discovering these things.

If people have discovered that they are driven to this search to find mystical openings for some kind of spiritual awareness, they traditionally try to find ways and means of allowing their inner cravings to somehow take form. They try to find ways to get them up and out of themselves and find a medium of expression. What people do if they are fortunate is to find an established group or teaching methods.

It was known that in order for a person to understand something of what lay ahead in the metaphysical path to enlightenment they had to first understand themselves. They had to understand and sort through their own identify and distinguish between those elements which were imposed by culture, and those elements which were genuine to them and those elements which were universal. This involved a tremendous amount of inner pain and searching because when you are trying to tell the difference between what is you and what is simply an appendage, the only way you can do it is to cut it and see if it bleeds. Artists who are working, whether in fiction, or the graphic arts, or in dance or anything else, know that if they are going to do something that has never been done before it has to be covered with their own blood. It has to be a thing that comes from a piece of their own flesh, taken out of the body and molded.

A master of such initiates would look at the images they dredge up from their subconscious and know instantly whether they were simply copying stuff that was in the air, whether they were taking designs from the wall, or whether they had found someone else's pictures. They would know whether this was their truth or not. If it was their truth this would have in fact been a masterpiece that would allow you to graduate and say, 'I know my own identity, I am free to do this.'

In attempting to find her identity, which is the Goddess, and find ways she could manifest, she apparently went down deep enough to get totally past Katelyn, to get totally past everything but her femininity, because these images are the Goddess.

Katelyn dug down deep enough to get past anything that is the person and found real legitimate expressions that came from such a mixed bag of a culture that it would be very difficult for her to have truly cheated. She does not know that some of these symbols are Babylonian, Sumerian, Chinese, and Welsh. She could not possibly have known without at least 10 or 15 years of study. She could not have made this mixed bag up by faking it. It has to come from someplace very real.

And therefore, I am extremely privileged to be here to be more or less the official midwife to announce to the world that this is not just an artist – Katelyn is an initiate of consciousness."

I have to admit even today it is hard for me to take all of that in and realize how connected I am to the energy of the Goddess. This is how the Goddess had awakened the divine feminine within me. We all have specific gifts that are unique and if we deny them we are denying our divine gifts. I believe visionary painting was the gift that was reactivated during my near-death experience in surgery to remove my intestines. I am just like you because we are all part of the divine, and I have gifts that are unique to me because I have something unique to share with the world. I am an initiate of feminine Goddess consciousness, and I am learning to embrace that. I am here to share that energy with the world and it is not an easy task to perform. I often wish I was just an ordinary girl living an ordinary life but the other part of me thinks that might be a bit boring for me.

My wellness returned when I began to acknowledge myself and listen to my Inner Physician. My health returned because I was doing things that made me feel good and disease can't live in an environment full of joy.

Even to this day, every time I spend time with those images or any of my visionary paintings they speak to me, always taking me to a deeper level with each viewing.

Let's explore how art and creative arts can facilitate well-being.

CREATIVE TECHNIQUE FOR WELLNESS

Creative Wellness

"When the artist is alive in any person, whatever his kind of work may be, he becomes an inventive, searching, daring, self-expressing, creature. He becomes interesting to other people. He disturbs, upsets, enlightens and he opens the way for a better understanding."

Robert Henri

Everyone is an artist. We are all co-creating our lives each and every day and that is a very creative process! Creative expression is essential to well-being and the lack of it is causing disease. For most people the creative process stops at about 10 years old when someone laughs at something we painted or the teacher tells us we can do a better job. Every time an attempt is made to draw something from that point on, we hear that laughter or the teacher's voice and we are a 10-year old who can't draw again. How many times have you heard someone say, "I can only draw stick people"? That is because it is only stick people who can squeeze through the crack in the door that is closed to creativity.

People in the flow of creative energy are open, flexible, spontaneous and fearless. They are willing to take risks, make mistakes and have fun in the process because it is in the risk and mistake-making that our greatest teachers live. In this flow of energy the whole world opens up and blesses you. When you are in creative space you are connected to your Source, which is Love. Love is the energy of well-being and the place where healing happens.

I have been a visionary artist and writer for many years. After years of practice I have learned to get out of my own way when I am creating and open to inspiration. I wish I could do the same during the creation of everyday life! As we learned in the chapter on breathing, the word inspire comes from the Latin word "inspirare" which means "to breathe into" or "in"-into "spirare," to breathe. Inspiration comes to us on the wings of the very breath we breathe. It can be just that easy if we are open and listening. Couple inspiration with imagination and you have manifestation. You get inspired, you imagine and have faith in a new future and it comes into manifestation.

We have learned about the importance of breathing consciously; now see how it is connected to creativity. The simple act of conscious breathing, deeply into the diaphragm, can be a meditation in itself and it can have a profound impact on the ability to creatively open up. Taoist master Mantak Chia describes the diaphragm as nothing less than a spiritual muscle. He says, "Lifting the heart and fanning the fires of digestion and metabolism, the diaphragm muscle plays a largely unheralded role in maintaining our health, vitality, and well-being."

How do we bring the artist alive as Robert Henri suggests in the above quotation? I believe that we can make sacred the space in our inner and outer environment using mind, body and spirit techniques, and from this sacred environment we are able to access our creative spirit. Creativity is born from the calm inner place that resides in the heart, not in the mind. It is the ability to invent, experiment, take risks, break rules, make mistakes and have fun doing it. We all have this ability and it is the stresses of life that make it difficult to access. From this space of innocence, imagination and play the door opens to our Inner Physician.

I trained in Mind-Body Medicine with Dr. James Gordon of the Center for Mind- Body Medicine in Washington D.C., the author of Manifesto for A New Medicine. He created a group model for stress release and relaxation that is simple and yet very powerful. Mind-Body Skills, including meditation, breathing techniques, movement, music, biofeedback, autogenic training, imagery, art and group processing, can all be thought of as forms of meditation. Over the past dozen years Dr. Gordon has used the techniques successfully with cancer patients and victims of war and torture. The successful use of the techniques is supported by research.

Dr. Gordon believes that awareness and meditation are fundamental to the deep change that is necessary for bringing about wellness. He says the following in 'Manifesto for a New Medicine: " Awareness allows us to see where we are; to stand for a moment outside ourselves; to appreciate in a powerful, personal way how the world around us affects us; to observe the thoughts, feelings, and sensations that arise in us. Meditation is a state of moment-to-moment awareness that over time may help to dissolve physical symptoms and habitual ways of thinking and acting. Both awareness and meditation enable us to experience the way our mind may limit or free us. Together they prepare us to use our mind to make the deep changes in thought, feeling, and action that are necessary for our healing."

These skills are so powerful I have integrated them in my creative process with much success, and so can you. Beginning with a simple breathing exercise, move into a shaking and dancing exercise to release stressful energy and end with a relaxed meditative state. These techniques create a clear space and inspiration flows because any stress has been removed so you become a receptive container. Within this sacred space you can connect with the wise inner guide, the inner well of creativity as well as the Inner Physician.

We each have our own unique form of creative expression. All we need to do to access this part of ourselves is step out of the way. For me mediation, music, journaling, movement and dance help me do that and open gateways to accessing my inner wise guide. I hope this inspires you to do the same.

AWAKENING YOUR INNER PHYSICIAN

Here is an exercise to help you clear yourself so you are open to the flow of creativity.

Breathing: Start with one of the breathing techniques you learned earlier. Do the breathing activity for 3-5 minutes.

Do this next part to the best of your ability. It should not be painful or uncomfortable. If you can't physically do the exercise the way it is presented get in a comfortable space, close your eyes and imagine you are doing it. This can be just as powerful as doing it physically because if you get into the imagery the mind is convinced that you are really doing it.

I use the Osho Kundalini and Dynamic Active Meditations CD for this part.

Shaking: After completing the breathing technique move into to the shaking activity. The purpose of this is to release tensions and break up physical and emotional patterns you might be holding. It will also raise your energy.

Plant your feet solidly on the ground/floor. Your eyes may be open or closed. Let your arms hang loose at your sides and make sure there is a slight bend in your knees. As the music begins, "shake" or bounce your body up and down, keeping your feet planted on the floor. Try to shake every part of your body from head to toe. If sound wants to come out let it come. Continue for 5-10 minutes.

Dancing: Now put on dance music that you like. It works best if you move seamlessly from one activity to the next so have your music ready to go.

Dance any way you feel and let your whole body move. Let your body lead you as you follow its cues. Pay attention to parts of your body that might be resistant. See if you can move into the resistance and let it be okay. If you can it will shift. Do this for 5-10 minutes.

Meditation: Close your eyes and be still. You can do this sitting or standing. Be the witness to your process and pay attention without focusing on what is happening inside and out. Let the thoughts float by like clouds as you acknowledge them and let them pass by. Do this for 10-15 minutes.

Resting: Now, keeping your eyes closed from the meditation, find a comfortable place to lie down and be still. Do this for 10-15 minutes.

Now you are ready to create! You can do this activity before doing any of the creative projects described in this book.

I have created a guided meditation called "The Body Scan" on Awakening the Inner Physician CD. The Body Scan is a Mind-Body-Spirit technique for exploring your body and discovering where it needs healing. You can order the CD at www.empoweredhealthandwellness.com.

CREATIVE TECHNIQUE FOR WELLNESS

Achieving Wellness Using Art

"Our study provides beginning evidence for the important role art therapy can play in reducing symptoms. Art therapy provides a distraction that allows patients to focus on something positive instead of their health for a time, and it also gives patients something they can control."

Judith Paice

Native traditions have used art throughout history to make tools for ritual, transformation and healing. These works of art are infused with a specific intention through the process of creating them and the intention is strengthened through the use of the object as it is incorporated into the ritual or used privately.

Visual expression was the first form of communication going back to cave painting. Before there was an alphabet man communicated with pictures.

In Australia the Aboriginal cosmology is that all life, whether it is human, animal, bird, mineral, fish or plant, is part of an unchanging interconnected system, one vast network of relationships that can be traced to the great Ancestor Spirits of the Dreaming. The heart and soul of the ancestors arise from the primitive images of their artwork and stories and they become the oracle that reveals their history. When we connect to our origins we are also in contact with our essence self, which is whole and complete. The essence self can lead us out of dis-ease and back to wholeness because it carries our blueprint for health. This is the realm of the Inner Physician.

Indigenous Australians lived by the information from what they called The Dreaming. They believed it linked them to their origins at the beginning of time. All over the world indigenous people still create art that is used in ritual to call forth spirit and connect intentionally to specific energy fields. Some of the works of art are used repeatedly while others are disposed of as part of the ritual.

Tibetan monks create beautiful sand mandalas whose sole purpose is to represent impermanence of all that exists and the cycles of life and death. This art is called dul-tson-kyil-khor, which literally means "mandala of colored powders." Millions of grains of sand are painstakingly laid into place on a flat platform over a period of days or weeks. I have watched monks create the sand mandalas working for hours to make sure every tiny detail is exact. The finished works are beautiful and they vanish in an instant as they are swept away through ritual. When finished the colored sands are gathered up and poured into a nearby river or stream where the waters carry the healing energies throughout the world.

In Ancient Egypt the final resting place was filled with intentional art. The body was carefully prepared and wrapped in a specific way and then placed in a sarcophagus that was highly decorated with symbols of the person's life and symbols that would assist them in their journey to the other world. The tomb itself was painted with scenes from the person's life and pictures of Gods who would protect them on their journey. When the ritual ceremony was completed the art was sealed so no one would see it, as it was created for the person who died and it was to remain sacred.

We have lost touch with the ancient form of creating intentional art, and it is through our reviving this tradition and seeing our creativity as a sacred act that we will be able to tap into this source of vast information that will guide our evolution. Begin today by being more mindful in your creative process and creating sacred space for the magic and mystery to dance. Everything exists in our imagination including perfect health and the process of making intentional art will set it free. Tap into your imagination and the Inner Physician and you will be amazed at what emerges to help you become well.

My post-baccalaureate degree is in art therapy and I know that art and wellness go hand in hand. I have used art with clients but for the most part art therapy has been my path to growth and transformation. As a visionary artist and trained art therapist I consider art making a key part of my spiritual path. I am very interested in the relationship between art and spirituality and how art making can be a path that assists the artist in conscious evolution. Art is a reflection of Spirit, both human and more-than-human.

Visual expression has been used for restoring health throughout history, but art therapy did not emerge as a distinct profession until the 1940s when artists working in psychiatric hospitals became aware that painting, drawing and other forms of artwork created the foundation for a therapeutic relationship between patient and therapist. The images that emerge from the unconscious reveal what is hidden and help the therapist gain a better understanding of the patient. It is the unconscious feelings and emotions that are creating disease and discomfort, so bringing them to light shifts perception. When I create a visionary image it is brought up from deep within me and often I see things that I would have never seen through another means that end up transforming me.

Art is an important medium for communication because it is less threatening for the client than talking directly about a problem. Art therapy interventions can be specifically designed to address problems so the client can integrate physical problems and emotional concerns, which is helpful because physical illness has an emotional component. In the same way, art can communicate with the artist and give them information about things they cannot see, such as illness and disease in the body. I have often finished a painting and upon observation discovered something about myself that had been hidden before the painting. This is one of the ways our Inner Physician communicates with us. Art therapy is a means for the patient to reconcile emotional conflicts, foster self-awareness, and express unspoken and frequently unconscious concerns about their disease and begin to have a dialog about them.

Carl Jung, the noted Swiss psychiatrist and psychotherapist and founder of analytical psychology, was known for his work with the mandala as well as visionary paintings in his own healing process and in working with clients. The mandala, which means 'circle' in Sanskrit, is a symbolic representation of the path to the center. The process of returning to center brings the body into balance. Creating mandalas can make the journey more meaningful and manageable, especially in the face of disease. Bonnie Bell, creator of the Gaia Star Mandalas said, "By gazing at a mandala, or by creating one ourselves, we tap into otherwise inaccessible sources of transformational help. Whether we understand these sources to be within ourselves or coming from spirit beyond, we can be greatly enlivened by their gifts. . . . I speak of this art with passion because I have been helped very deeply by contemplating and creating mandalas. During a recent health crisis that could not really be addressed by allopathic medicine, these images have been a constant source of comfort and inspiration. In a very real way, I have drawn on mandalas as a source of 'beauty-medicine.'"

Mandalas are a form of intentional art, which is an object created with a specific intention. By infusing the artwork with intention we strengthen the focus that we are working on. As the artist, we set a focus before creating the piece and infuse it with the spirit of the intention through the art making process. Art that is made with intention becomes medicine for the spirit and nourishment for the soul. For example, I made both a healing doll and a medicine pouch to take on a pilgrimage to Mexico and they have become powerful healing tools for me.

Art can be created to strengthen the energy around any intention, such as creating prosperity, healing a specific illness, manifestation, or bringing a partner into your life. If the artist can create space that is sacred and step out of their own way, spirit will speak through them into the piece they are creating. The intention is strengthened by using it in ritual, by placing in on an altar or using it in meditation. Each piece has a spirit and radiance which speaks to the soul and can be used for personal healing or in healing work with other people. The Universe hears the request and comes to support that desire to heal on the physical plane. This act also engages the Inner Physician. I have made intentional art for myself as well as for others who have needed images of healing.

When I am in creative space, mystery unfolds before my eyes, and if I am able to step out of my way I create images that are a reflection of something bigger, such as the images of the Goddess I painted. The process of creating art has taught me to relinquish my need to control and understand, so that I can connect with mystery and listen to its wisdom. Each piece of intentional art is created through an intuitive connection. If I am working with a client I connect with the client's inner being and wise one. I gather the information and create an object specific to the healing needs of the client, through dolls, soul portraits, shamanic rattles, medicine bags and portable shrines.

Visionary art making, whether it is writing, visual art, dance or music, is a shamanic process. Many artists have enhanced powers of seeing, hearing and dreaming which allow them move easily between the worlds without experiencing the boundaries that keep others from exploring those realms. The artist often takes this journey for self-exploration but the images, movement, songs and poems that result are transformational, enlightening, healing and empowering to those who experience their work.

Collage is a simple form of creating intentional art, using material found around the house, such as magazines, old greeting cards, scissors and glue. It becomes more elaborate and complex with the addition of other materials, such as old photos, ribbons, buttons, wrapping paper and other ephemera. Collage is defined as "An artistic composition of flat materials, magazine and newspaper clippings, fabric and objects pasted on a surface, often with unifying lines and color, such as a picture background."

Early examples of paper collage are the works of twelfth-century Japanese calligraphers, who prepared surfaces for their poems by gluing paper and fabric scraps to create a background on which to letter. Many of the techniques used today are inspired by ancient collage techniques. Art historians generally attribute the first use of collage in fine art to Pablo Picasso, who incorporated oilcloth into a cubist still life in 1912.

The creation of a collage or vision board made with collage can be a vehicle for insight, healing and expanded consciousness. By allowing yourself to select images and materials intuitively and spontaneously put them together, the finished image will bring up information from the unconscious, which you might not have been aware of. The images that you choose are images that have called to your unconscious and reflect something your soul wants you to see.

Mix imagination and intuition with a group of powerful cut-out images and you will give voice to your soul and bring information to your awareness so you can explore its contents. What you are doing as you search for images and material is finding parts of yourself, kind of like an artistic soul retrieval. Some images you choose will be familiar and others will be mysterious and mythic. The mysterious, mythic images represent archetypes that have chosen you who want to speak to you. The completed collage will have a story to tell that is just for you.

I created a series of 75 collage images on cards that explore the mythic journey, which I now use to do intuitive readings. They create a journey of the inner landscape of the person who is having the reading. Though the images don't change, they tell a different story, depending on the client and the issues they are dealing with. Clients are always amazed at how accurate the information from the cards is. When anyone creates a collage for healing you will find the same accuracy emerge if it comes from a connection with your Inner Physician.

Here is an activity which will help you explore collage making and create an image that will support your return to health. When it is complete put it in a place where you will see it every day. This image will speak to your soul and activate your Inner Physician. In the resource section of the book you will find a web address where I create personal healing images that you can work with if you don't want to create your own. These are very powerful healing images that impact people for years.

AWAKENING YOUR INNER PHYSICIAN

You might want to create a collage deck about your wellness journey. Create a series of cards as a symbol of where you are, where you are going and where you want to end up. When you feel challenged create a card that is about overcoming that challenge. Use the images for journaling or for daily visualization. You can create as many cards as your journey requires. You can create a path leading back to your healthy self, using the collage image series.

Think of an intention you would like to focus on. Gather magazines and begin looking through them to find pictures and words that speak to you about your intention. You will use them to create a collage that will be placed in a prominent place in your room where you will see it every day on a shrine that is created to focus the intention.

Think of your intention when you start the activity and then let it go. As you go through the magazines, select images that call to you and set them in a pile. When you feel you have enough images, start to create your collage. You can use card stock cut to 3 x 5 inches or the size of your choice for your base. Take the images, cut off the excess paper and put them together with other images to create your cards. You might be surprised at the final images and they might have information to share with you that you didn't have access to before. Try this as an experiment and see if you are able to see movement toward your intention after a couple of weeks.

You may choose to do a series of collages to explore a particular issue. As you create the series, moving from image to image, you are going deeper. As you descend, patterns will emerge and within the patterns the answers to your query will be revealed. You might want to purchase a journal with blank pages, create a collage, let the image speak to you through writing and then move to the next collage and repeat the process until you feel your process has come to completion. When your collage cards are finished you can continue to work with them by selecting one each day and using it as a meditation.

One more place I want to explore with you in this chapter is the Medicine Woman and how her energy can be a journey of wellness if you work with her.

CREATIVE TECHNIQUE FOR WELLNESS

The Path of the Medicine Woman

"The call to power necessitates a separation from the mundane world: the neophyte turns away from the secular life, either voluntarily, ritually, or spontaneously through sickness, and turns inward towards the unknown, the mysterium. This change of direction can be accomplished only through what Carl Jung has referred to as 'an obedience to awareness.'"

Joan Halifax, The Wounded Healer

I include the Medicine Woman here because not only is she connected to the

Goddess but she is an archetype for restoring health. The Medicine Woman is a female shaman and it is traditionally a calling, which a woman receives either when she is young from her elders or through a healing crisis.

Her purpose is to assist members of the community in healing and she acts as an intermediary between ordinary and non-ordinary reality. Shamanism is an ancient method of communication that is used for spiritual and physical healing as well as personal growth. The work of the Medicine Man/Woman/Shaman is to communicate through a journey to the natural and supernatural worlds and with the universal energy that unites us and bring back the wisdom they discover. In the journey the shaman encounters helping spirits, in the form of animals, angels, ancestors and ascended masters, who are consciousness that does not exist in a body. The spirits provide help and guidance when properly approached and acknowledged. Shamanic practices exist in many tribal cultures around the world and we are experiencing a renaissance in urban cultures as people realize the power of this ancient healing art.

Many shamans are also artists who create paintings, carvings, music, sound, dance and story about the visions they discover in other realms. I consider my artwork shamanic because of how it is created and how it is healing to those who see it. When I speak of shamanic art making I am not speaking of drug induced art making but art that comes out of a shamanic journeying process. Shamans create a sound field that changes consciousness using drums and rattles, which assist them in entering an altered mental state, something I have done in my visionary art. It is not a matter of going somewhere "out there" but learning how to travel the inner landscape, the world of the dream. The act of traveling, going in, receiving and retrieving are feminine functions whether you are male or female.

In The Woman in the Shaman's Body, Barbara Tedlock goes far beyond arguing that women and men have held equal roles with one another in indigenous shamanism. She devotes the second half of her book to documenting a vital concept that has been consistently ignored or downplayed by male anthropologists – the idea "that women's bodies and minds are particularly suited to tap into the power of the transcendental." She proposes that "female hormones play a central role in women's shamanic abilities" and that "within the dark fluids of menstrual and birthing blood resides the vital essence of the most feminine form of spiritual energy." She also suggests that women experience their strongest healing and oracular powers just before and during menstruation. That is why women were often separated from Native American rituals when menstruating. It wasn't because they were weak but because their energy was too strong for ritual space. "Mood swings and heightened sensitivity at this time of the month – which in the West have been labeled premenstrual syndrome (PMS) and treated as an illness – are actually manifestations of an altered state of consciousness made possible by female biology."

The indigenous healing path is very dear and familiar to me and I am sure I have had numerous lifetimes as a medicine person in different parts of the world. I have been drawn to it since I was a child and I saw people from the Outback of Australia on National Geographic. When my spiritual path opened up 30 years ago I entered it through the Native American healing traditions and my first teacher was a Cherokee Medicine Woman. I have studied with both male and female shamans from South America, in particular Chile and Peru. In this lifetime my medicine path includes creating healing art as well as practicing the shamanic arts. Both practices require going into other realms and returning with information and wisdom to use in healing.

In some ways Native healing arts can be compared to psychology so it is no surprise that I was also drawn to that field. Clarissa Pinkola Estes, Ph.D., says, "The word 'psychology' literally means the study of the life of the soul. The word 'psyche' is derived from the ancient word 'prushke' which is related to both the image of 'la mariposa' the butterfly and 'la alma' the soul. The word is also related to the essence of the breath; in other words, to the animating force without which all of us would lie dead upon the ground. 'Psychology' in its truest sense is not the study of behavior per se, but the study of the animating force. The same is also true in curanderismo." I saw myself as more of a medicine woman and less of a therapist when I was practicing psychology because I had a holistic and less traditional approach to doing therapy with my clients, using art therapy, sound and music therapy, movement, play and dreaming as well as my intuition.

Curanderismo is a medicine path that is the art of folk healing by a curandero (or curandera for a female), the healer par excellence who is a traditional folk healer or shaman in Latin America. It is a path that is dedicated to curing physical and/or spiritual illnesses. It includes various techniques such as prayer, herbal medicine, healing rituals, spiritualism, massage, and psychic healing. Healers can be either male or female and may even specialize in their practice. Curanderismo comes from the Spanish word "cura" which means "to heal" or "to be a priest."

Indigenous healing arts deal with the negative and positive principles of the psyche as well as taking into account the stories of a person's life, their dreams, mundane life and the environment and investigating the life of the soul in depth. The mind, soul and spirit are not seen as separate from the body, and nature and the person's environment are all considered in the holistic view that the medicine man or woman takes. It has been Western medicine that has compartmentalized man and the healing process causing a great deal of inner separation which makes healing more difficult.

At this point I want to leave the Medicine Man behind and focus my attention on the Medicine Woman, because I can speak to that from my own experience. As Tedlock suggests, the medicine path for women is different from that of men. By our nature, the female body is attuned with the cycles of the cosmos in a way that the male body is not. For example women bleed with the moon cycles and therefore are very connected to the phases the moon moves through. Bleeding and birthing are shamanic events that men do not have access to. Women gather information, process it and share it with others differently than men and that is an important distinction between the two paths. As a woman our first nature is the feminine, even though we contain both masculine and feminine processes.

Medicine Women have existed for thousands of years and still exist throughout the world traditionally holding the secrets to healing magic. Though the path has been hidden for centuries and even now many female shamans do their work in private, it is a very powerful path. Woman is by nature a shaman, says a Chukchee proverb from Siberia, and many traditions say that the first shaman was female.

The earliest known female shaman was that of a woman of the Upper Paleolithic age about 30,000 years ago. During the time of the Inquisition women and women's healing wisdom were forced underground. Much of this ancient knowledge was purged from our societies over thousands of years and culminated in the burning of "witches" around the world. We were taught to fear women's healing wisdom or discount it as irrational. The connection with nature, the knowledge of plants and herbs, and the intuition to hone in on problem areas were gifts that became feared by those who did not possess them. It was safer to discount their validity than to see them as valuable assets to the healing process. Medicine women fled to the mountains or hid in the back of their kitchens to practice their healing arts, keeping below the negative radar. Women are healing past lives as "witches" who were burned at the stake or hanged for practicing healing wisdom.

Every woman is connected to the Medicine Woman because of our ability to give birth and heal our young, but not every woman is called to the Medicine Woman path as a healer. Inside each woman is a being of wisdom, deeply connected to the phases of the moon, the tides of the sea, and the changing seasons. If we trust that innate wisdom it will guide us.

A woman by nature takes on many roles, and often feels as if there are many different things happening inside of her all at once. The medicine woman is artist, poet, dreamer, midwife, cook, intuitive, dancer, storyteller and curious explorer and something is always birthing inside of her. The shamanic arts of healing, divination, communing with the elements of nature including animals, intuitive arts and dream interpretation, drumming, being oracles, shape shifting, and ecstatic dancing have been part of this natural profession held by women for thousands of years.

Women read energy fields through the emotional body as we merge with Mother Earth. The shamanic medicine path for women is deep, intuitive, spontaneous, flexible, open and creative, and allowing and dreaming is our nature. Healing, birthing children, gathering and growing food, keeping communities in balance, presiding over ceremonies and rites of passage, maintaining relations with the dead, teaching, ministering to those in need, communing with nature to learn her secrets, preserving the wisdom traditions, divining the future, and dancing with Gods and Goddesses are all shamanic arts of women.

In recent years there has been an increased interest and awareness in indigenous healing. Many people hunger to become more connected to the earth and natural healing methods in countries like the US where it has more than disappeared. More recently the art of being a Medicine Woman has been revived and is gaining respect as a viable medicine path. There are more practicing Medicine Women alive today than ever before using the natural ways of their ancestors in combination with new technology that has been developed. There are herbalists, naturalists, aromatherapists, massage therapists, and those who teach spirituality, awareness, and meditation skills. In some respects the field of psychology can be seen as a medicine path when looking at transpersonal psychology which works with people on a holistic level. The shamanic path of training and apprenticeship is populated mainly by men and while much wisdom can be gained from these teachers it is important for women to be able to study with female Medicine Women in groups of women, too. I always felt I was coming more from the Medicine Woman in me when I practiced therapy, using my intuition and holding space for healing and transformation to happen naturally for my clients.

AWAKENING YOUR INNER PHYSICIAN

Are you a healer like any of the ones mentioned above? Of course you are because we all are to some extent. It is a matter of tapping in, tuning in and turning on. If you have an interest and feel a connection with the healing arts of the Medicine Woman it might be the perfect vehicle to support your healing process. You may want to find a Medicine Woman to work with or you might want to study shamanism yourself. There are many great books to read including The Woman in the Shaman's Body.

When we are in a healing process from an illness or disease it is hard to be objective so finding someone who is a Medicine Man or Woman rather than studying it yourself might be the best way to go for now. I used a combination of healing myself using medicine techniques I had learned while studying shamanism and eliciting the help of practicing Medicine Women. It was a more difficult path than putting myself totally in the hands of a healer because I had to find my objectivity while also working with wounded parts of myself that had a tendency to sabotage. For someone who doesn't have experience in the shamanic arts now is not the best time to begin to explore them. You can learn a lot about the shamanic arts by being the receiver of their healing gifts, possibly more than you might learn through study. You can go back and study after you are healthy.

I lead groups of women to Chile to work with Luzclara, a Chilean Medicine Woman in Santiago once a year. If you are interested in learning more e-mail me.

CHAPTER SIX

Milagros for Wellness

"The word Milagro means 'miracle' in Spanish. Milagros are small religious charms, which some believe have spiritual or magical powers for healing. If one prays with a Milagro, some believe it can help restore and preserve wellbeing and balance in their lives or the people they pray for. People might carry a Milagro with them to reap its benefit such as curing a physical ailment or to ward off evil or bring about change or fortune."

Author Unknown

When I first read about Milagros the idea fascinated me and resonated with my Inner Physician. Milagros are votive offerings used to request healing, which look like small gold and silver charms shaped like body parts, animals, cars, houses and other objects. They are hung on the images of Christ, Mary and the saints in churches all over Mexico by people asking for healing or giving thanks for healing that has been granted. Statues are literally covered with these charms, and of photos of people requesting healing. I resonate with the idea of a charm that represents healing a certain part of the body and using it as an offering, because it creates a visual to focus on. I was happy to find that I could buy them outside many of the churches in Mexico as well as on the internet.

Using Milagros is an ancient custom in the Hispanic world that goes back to between the fifth and first century before Christ by Iberians who lived in the coastal regions of Spain. You can find bronze Milagros, almost identical to the contemporary ones, in Spain's archaeological museums. Milagros as votive offerings accompanied the Spanish into the New World and their use has been documented in nearly all areas of the Hispanic Americas. Today the ritual appears to be connected to Christianity, though ancient beliefs and practices are still active in Spanish speaking people and might be part of the ritual.

There is a new use for Milagros springing up in New Mexico these days. If a friend is about to have an eye operation, the gift of an eye Milagro helps to say,

"I wish you well." A pair of lungs can say, "I hold space for your lungs to be well." An arm and a leg given to a couple trying to buy a house can wish them good luck obtaining financing. An ear Milagro can suggest that someone be a better listener. An ax Milagro might suggest that a relationship should end. The Milagros are a special way to tell someone you support their path and well-being.

For the men out there who are reading this book, I would like to warn you in advance that this chapter is pretty graphic in terms of the female body. You might want to close your eyes and not look at the images I create with my words. I want the reader to fully understand what I experienced and how I transformed it so the details are important.

In December of 1998 when I was diagnosed with a prolapsed womb, I saw four doctors and each of them told me told me I would not get better and the only solution was to have a hysterectomy. My Inner Physician did not agree. I set on a journey that would lead me to sacred ground where the indigenous peoples worshiped the Goddess for thousands of years but also to the sacred ground inside of myself where I would come face to face with the hidden parts of myself that were blocking my health.

I was disappointed as I encountered a school of thought in the medical community that believes women's body parts are disposable when it comes to uteruses, ovaries and breasts. I also encountered an attitude that when we pass childbearing age those parts serve no function and it is easier to remove them than try to heal them – in essence just chop them off and throw them away! This discounts the facts that there are structural and energetic reasons for the uterus since it has hormonal functions and that the womb is the home of creativity in women. When I say creativity I don't just mean creating children, but also the children of our dreams and our creative imagination.

The lack of support I experienced is the very thing that leads women to disown parts of themselves, to struggle with self-acceptance and to feel somehow less valued. For hundreds of years women have struggled against these beliefs as they have tried to gain equal footing with men. We have made progress in a lot of areas but in the area of physical acceptance the average woman still struggles. We reject our bodies, we reject our looks, we reject our intelligence and we reject our physical abilities.

The treatment I experienced throughout the process of saving my uterus was painful, non-supportive and degrading, and it all came from women doctors who I would have hoped would have been able to have compassion for the female experience. Unfortunately they have been trained

144

in a male-dominated field using antiquated understandings of the female body.

Finding one's uterus protruding from the vagina is a frightening thing by itself and being treated poorly adds to the trauma. The doctor I saw in the after-hours Urgent Care Clinic told me I would need a hysterectomy and it was no big deal because I didn't need my uterus any longer. She poked, prodded and looked at my vaginal area from all different angles including me lying down, sitting up and standing with my legs spread apart while she looked up from the floor. I can assure you that it was as embarrassing as it sounds. She took a piece of paper and wrote "Uterine prolapsed with cervix protruding through the vagina." She gave it to me and told me to read it to the person who sets up appointments at my clinic. I wasn't sure how serious this condition was and my question went unanswered for two weeks because that was the soonest I could get in to see a doctor. Even the person making the appointment said it was no big deal that my uterus was falling out. It was to me! Who trains these people, for gosh sake?

While waiting two weeks for the appointment I went back and forth about keeping my uterus or having it removed. Through the process I came face to face with my sense of vulnerability, the fear of surgery and possible loss of life, my feelings of inadequacy and a great sense of loss, as I realized my body would never be the same and that I would lose that part of me which was once the home of my children. With that thought my inner warrior kicked in and I made a commitment to bring my body back into harmony even though I was told that wouldn't happen. I researched and tried a long list of alternative methods for healing the womb including acupuncture, herbs, imagery, crystals taped to my abdomen, and exercise. Some of the things had an impact, others didn't seem to work at all. I was disappointed that I couldn't change my condition and almost gave into the inevitable.

After two weeks I finally saw a gynecologist who was a young woman with a condescending attitude and no compassion or sensitivity. She chuckled to herself as I told her I was trying herbs and acupuncture to help my uterus. She listened to my report of what happened and looked at me and said, "It must have been hanging out for a long time and you just didn't notice it. They don't just fall out like that!" I know my body and I know it hadn't been hanging out for a long time like she was suggesting. This doctor also poked and prodded me and looked up my vagina from all angles just like the first doctor. I knew from her attitude that she was not someone I could form an alliance of wellness with, so I kept all of my questions to myself.

I told her I didn't want a hysterectomy. She told me I didn't really need one but I didn't need my uterus either. She told me a pessary would hold it in place just fine. A pessary is a fairly hard, pink rubber disk with a hole in it that fits inside the vaginal canal and keeps the uterus from falling out. The doctor left the room and returned with a pessary and said, "This one is too big for you, but I don't have your size and I don't have the time to fit you. If it bothers you just take it out." She put this 4-inch disk into my already traumatized body and left the room. I was not given instructions on how to take it out, how to clean it or how to get it back in. Everything I read later stressed the importance of careful fitting so they are comfortable. By the time I got to the parking lot I was in extreme pain. I won't go into the details of how I removed it aside from saying it was not a pretty sight. I put the damn thing in a drawer where it remains to this day. Can you see why I was now on a path to prove all of these doctors wrong?

Next, I was referred to a specialist to talk to her about having a hysterectomy even though I said I didn't want one and planned to keep my uterus where it was. She examined me in the same embarrassing way as the other doctors did and said, "It is so low that if I had the right instruments I could yank it out right now." If she had had pliers I think she might have just pulled it right out of me then and there! I was shocked by the insensitivity and said, "No thank you, I am keeping it," and I left. In my case, it was important that I keep it and not have it removed. This might not be true for every woman but it was important for me.

Saving my uterus now became like a political stand for me, as I was faced with doctors who had more interest in efficiency and removing "the no longer needed organ." I became a womb warrior. A part of my body that I had previously paid little attention to, I am sad to say, now became the object of daily focus. Images and metaphors of the womb began to show up everywhere and permeate my life. Through the process my womb taught me a deep, deep level of appreciation for the meaning of being a woman and about the magic, mystery and creativity of womb space, as I wrote poetry and created paintings to tell its story. I had conversations with my womb and gained deep wisdom about what it means to be a woman. I learned that being a woman is an honor and a blessing and not a curse. Yes a curse. I was raised in a generation where men were honored and women were treated like second-class citizens. This was certainly true in my family and from the treatment I was receiving from the medical community that sense was reinforced.

With the lack of support from my doctors I had to rely on my inner conviction.

Through much of the process I would become polarized as I tried to hold my vision for a healthy uterus and the physical evidence was telling me it wasn't occurring. It became clear to me that I had to go below the physical level, into the emotional, cellular level to find answers and until I could discover the underlying issues I would probably not get better.

It was this dance of duality within me that took me on the deep inner journey to discover all of the places that I was rejecting myself. The medical model was providing a metaphor for me to see how I was unconsciously buying into beliefs that parts of me didn't have value. The inner demons that were keeping me in disharmony had voices; they came through my family, society and the media. They told me I was not beautiful, that I was not good enough, that there was something wrong with me and that it wasn't ok to be a woman and they were speaking loud and clear. Listening to them caused me to reject in a real, physical sense the most creative part of my body, my womb.

The physical manifestation of my uterine prolapse was giving me gifts. As I pushed past negative beliefs about myself I discovered a deep inner beauty. I began to cherish the fact that I was a woman, and to love my body just as it is for it is the temple I created to carry me through this journey. I learned that my body is very wise and can return to homeostasis on its own if I get out of the way. I met my Inner Physician and got guidance along the way.

For well over a year and a half I focused on my uterus. I discovered that its health lay in letting go of the fear of what might happen, acceptance of where my body was in its process and trust in myself and the Loving Creator. It is so difficult to let go when the body is involved. So much fear comes up about the unknown and how your body might be impacted. My vivid imagination had a field day exploring all the morbid possibilities.

I was drawn to Our Lady of Guadalupe, as an ancient image of the Divine Feminine, and bought a beautiful statue of her for my shrine of wellness. A few days after I bought her I woke one morning to find her shattered on the floor in a number of pieces, the apparent victim of one of my cats. The main break went around the circumference of the statue at the level of her womb. When I saw her broken body on the floor tears started to come into my eyes but I could not cry. I felt a shock wave go through my own body that transcended the sadness as I had a sense that when the statue broke something also broke loose in me. Memory ran through me of my past, in this life and other lives.

I realized as I stood there that she broke so that I could repair her just as I could repair myself. I carried the pieces upstairs to my studio and she practically put herself together in such a way one would never know she had broken. Paint that I mixed matched perfectly the first time and cracks filled in effortlessly. Before I repaired her I put crystals and a prayer inside of her hollow space, her womb. By afternoon I was experiencing excruciating pain in a "belt" around my body in the same area she had broken. The pain lasted for about 10 hours and then disappeared. I experienced this pain 2 other times during my trip to Mexico. The process of releasing density and trauma from the body can be painful and look like lack of process when it really is progress.

In December 2000, I took a pilgrimage to Mexico to visit the Goddess Guadalupe. I planned the trip so that I would be there for the Feast of Our Lady of Good Health so I could leave Milagros and ask for healing. I talk more about the pilgrimage in a later chapter. While there I visited many churches, left Milagros for friends, family and myself and was renewed by the faith of the Mexican People. My pilgrimage began at the Basilica of Our Lady of Good Health in Patzcuaro and ended at The Villa of Guadalupe in Mexico City, where I asked the Divine Mother to support my wellness. As I made an all day journey to The Villa of Our Lady of Guadalupe, in Mexico City, I felt my connection to the Mother strengthening. I had been "taken" to Mexico to reunite with my true Mother who I felt disconnected from since I was a young girl, and now The Goddess was asking me to trust her! Trust at this point was difficult for me to maintain.

I was pushed to the edge of surrender as my fear of being let down by the Mother grew stronger and my anger about lack of support rose. The feelings were a response from early childhood and maternal abandonment that occurred when I was four that I hadn't faced. I surrendered, knowing this was a gateway to my wellness. I plunged into the part of me that felt totally separated, totally alone, helpless and immobilized. I feared I could not take care of myself, in the way a four-year-old might experience that fear if abandoned by its mother. I was afraid I would stay in this space forever.

The feelings were heightened by the fact that I was a couple of thousand miles from home, alone in a foreign country, where I couldn't speak the language and I was facing my biggest fear. The experience lasted for days as I witnessed all of the parts of myself that I was still rejecting take the spotlight so I could see and accept them.

This was a deep transformation that needed to take place because when I was four, I went into a seizure as a result of a high fever due to an ear infection, and was hospitalized for five days. During those five days my mother did not visit me and not only did I feel abandoned but I feel I made an unconscious commitment to be independent so I wouldn't have to feel this kind of rejection again. I had become a master of independence to the point that I felt I didn't need anyone. This needed to change.

In my darkest moment I was surrounded by a presence that I could feel physically as a tingling in my entire body. I felt "hands" cradling the sides of my head and that sensation stayed with me for an entire day. I began to understand at a core level that I was not alone nor had I ever been. The presence carried me back to that part of me which is light and love and I was filled with a sense of trust and peace like I had never felt before. I became trust and it was no longer something outside of me that I couldn't reach, it was in me. I began to see the beauty in the gift that my body gave me even though it has been filled with pain, suffering and discomfort.

I had turned a corner toward self-love. My struggle with self-acceptance was beginning to lose its grip on me and in turn I was beginning to love my body for the first time in my life. In this space my womb could do what it needed to so it could move back where it belonged in my body.

As I drove to the doctor for my annual physical, I reflected on my experience of the year before. My doctor had looked at me as if I was crazy when I told her I was going to heal myself using alternative therapies and she shook her head and rolled her eyes as I recounted the things I had already tried. Her exam revealed that I had made no progress. As I was getting ready to leave, her parting words to me were, "You know you will never get better and you will call me when you are ready for your hysterectomy." I left her office and cried all the way home.

After my grand cry my sense of resolve returned and once again I put my foot down and said no to the doctor's proclamation. I shifted my thoughts and began to think about having a healthy uterus again. It really bothers me when doctors say things that don't support the process of wellness. I know it comes from an old belief that they don't want to get our hopes up, but that is the very thing we need to do if we are going to heal. We need to have high hopes and faith in the co-creative process. I don't know if the doctor realized it but she was planting a seed, and if I was in the place of accepting it, it is very possible it would have grown and I would have believed it too. Though her words

153

challenged me I held on to my resolve to have a healthy uterus again. I spent another year focusing on a healthy uterus and using creative ways to make that happen. Some of you might be reading this saying, "Just let it go and have it removed," but that wasn't an option for me because it was important to my transformation to keep it. As you can see, when I put my mind to something it is hard to change it.

I went to my physical the following year with dread because I feared it would just reinforce the fact that I wasn't making progress. I was concerned that she would say I hadn't changed and it would prove that all my hard work and positive thinking had been a waste of time like it had been the year before. The seed the doctor planted still nibbled on me unconsciously. On my way to the doctor I prayed to Guadalupe to use me as an example to show the doctor that there are other ways to help the body. I didn't want anyone else to experience what I had.

My doctor asked me how I felt my uterus was doing and I responded, "I believe it is better." Upon examination she was shocked to find that my womb had moved more than three inches and it was almost back in its normal position. It was exciting to watch her perspective change right in front of me and it was affirming to come to a place of support and respect with her.

Radical trust led me to the place within that can experience miracles and the intention for the miracle began as a prayer attached to a tiny gold Milagro, left at the shrine of Our Lady. Even now, 16 years after my diagnosis, I still have my uterus and I am pain free. When I go for my physical these days the doctor doesn't even mention my uterus except to say it looks very healthy.

If one other woman can have a more supportive response because my body has resolved this problem and be given options because the doctor saw a new possibility, then my pain and discomfort have been worth it. I believe we have choices and options in all situations. They can vary from believing you can return to health, or that you should try something else or just surrender to what is. If it is a choice made out of self-love and we commit to it, the entire Universe comes in to support us and shines a light on the path that will lead to wholeness.

I couldn't have made this journey without the Inner Physician coming into partnership with me. Discovering this partnership, finding my beauty as a woman, and gaining trust and self-acceptance were the gifts I gathered in the process. I believe that healing came about because I stopped questioning the voice of the Inner Physician in me that knows what is best for me even if others might not agree. I had choices all along the way and the ones that I made out of love rather than out of fear were the ones that carried me.

CREATIVE TECHNIQUE
FOR WELLNESS

Power of the Pilgrimage

"As I make my slow pilgrimage through the world, a certain sense of beautiful mystery seems to gather and grow."

Arthur Christopher Benson

Man has been going on pilgrimages for thousands of years, with the first pilgrimage being accorded to Abraham, some 4000 years ago. Many of the destinations that draw pilgrims are shrines to specific holy people or sites of ancient civilizations which are known for their healing energies. Taking a pilgrimage for healing is a transformational experience!

I was at The Women and Spirituality Conference in Mankato, Minnesota one year and attended a workshop about a woman's pilgrimage to Spain to walk the Camino. Her workshop inspired me and made me feel it would be important to share a pilgrimage that I took because it was an integral part of my healing journey.

A pilgrimage is a prayer set in motion. Going on a pilgrimage begins with a commitment to go to a sacred place, in a conscious and prayerful way, for the purpose of healing and/or renewal. When a person makes the commitment, the Universe steps in to support that journey, lining things up with grace and ease which might not fall into place in ordinary circumstances. From the commitment stage through preparation, entering the journey and integrating upon their return, the person is never the same.

My pilgrimage began in May of 2000 with a spontaneous comment to my roommate that I was going to visit 50 Catholic churches before my next birthday. I didn't know this would be the beginning of a pilgrimage. I had a feeling when the words tumbled out of my mouth I was in for something bigger but I had no idea what that would be. My intention was to be with The Virgin Mary, whom I experience as feminine consciousness, and ask for healing for my womb which had prolapsed. The idea of going to Catholic churches was unusual because I had left the church when I was 14 and had not been in church since. I had unresolved issues with the dogma of Catholicism and my experience as a child in Catholic school. On the other hand I had the sense that the energy of The Virgin Mary was what I needed.

I began spending time in meditation in front of statues of Mary in various churches near my home. I would go at times when I knew no one would be there because I wanted to be in sacred space undisturbed. I was surprised to find so many of the churches were locked at times when one would think they would be open. When I did manage to get into a church I felt like I didn't belong there. It was a similar feeling to how I felt as a child in church.

The frustration of going to so many churches and finding them locked made me decide to take a different path to fulfill the goal. I started by researching information about The Virgin Mary, which quickly lead me to Our Lady of Guadalupe, Mary Magdalene, Sophia and other representations of the Black Madonna. I felt great affinity with the Black Madonnas and Guadalupe in particular, because they were more earthy and human than the Virgin Mary who is portrayed as pure, perfect and less than human.

The pull toward Our Lady of Guadalupe was strong and it was clear that I was to go to churches in Mexico to find healing. Researching places where miraculous healing occurred pointed me in many directions. My first instinct was the Shrine of Our Lady of Guadalupe in Mexico City which I quickly dismissed when I learned that hundreds of thousands of people went there each year and I was looking for solitude. I discovered a town in Central Mexico called Patzcuaro, a colonial city in the heart of the Sierra Madres which is known as" the place of entrance to Divinity," The patron saint of Patzcuaro is Our Lady of Health (Nuestra Señora de la Salud), an aspect of The Virgin Mary, who is said to do miraculous healing. She is represented by a beautiful statue, created in the 16th century, modeled from maize (corn) paste and crushed lotus petals and painted like a real person. She is housed in The Basilica of Our Lady of Health and on December 8th, which is her feast day, pilgrims come from all over Mexico to pray for healing. I was determined to be in the Basilica on her feast day to request healing for my womb.

Searching the internet for places to stay in Patzcuaro, I stumbled on a web site for a foundation that gave fellowships to artists to stay in a 250-year-old monastery right in town a few blocks from the Basilica. I applied and was awarded a fellowship to go to Patzcuaro to paint for the month of December. The Universe was not only supporting my commitment to heal but also my commitment to do my artwork at the same time.

I decided to create a doll that would represent wellness and health for me that I could take with me. Intention is strengthened for me if I create a visual object that acts as a symbol of the intention. I created a powerful healing doll, placing my hair, stones and crystals and other objects in her body as I meditated and prayed my intention into her to animate my request. My vision was to leave the doll at the shrine.

My travel from my home in Minnesota to Patzcuaro took me ten hours by plane, taxi and bus and another taxi, to reach my destination. It was challenging to be alone and not know the language. The last hour of travel took place in a taxi which got lost in the dark of night. I wrote the address where I was staying on an index card and gave it to the driver when I got into the taxi. He drove through parts of Patzcuaro that were dark and foreboding, down alleys and up streets. After an hour of this he stopped the car, got out and ran up to a church. For the first time in the journey I was afraid. I thought that if I didn't come up with something I would be dumped in the dark, empty street to find my own way so I got out of the car. When the driver returned I pointed to the trunk of the car and said "telephone," the only English word I thought he might understand. He opened the trunk and I took my backpack and poured the contents on the sidewalk to find the letter I had received from the fellowship sponsor with the address on it. He read the address, smacked himself in the forehead and drove me right where I needed to go. This is the kind of challenge that makes a pilgrimage transformational. You must learn to rely on yourself and trust that you are guided and protected.

I arrived in Patzcuaro on December 1, 2000 just as the entire town was beginning the week-long process of preparing for the largest holiday festival of the year, the day dedicated to Our Lady of Health. I set up a shrine in my room at the monastery and dedicated it to Our Lady and my healing, using my doll as the centerpiece. When I travel I like to create a shrine in my room to make the space sacred for me. I do this by bringing with me things that are sacred such as stones, small statues and figurines and anything that represents a current issue I am exploring or something I want to create in my life. I find a table or dresser space and set up my sacred space using those things. Once I do this I feel protected and the space has a connection to my home.

The first time I went to the Basilica and saw the statue of Our Lady, her beauty stunned me. She was almost life size, with long brown human hair and real clothes and jewelry. With over 400 years of prayer and dedication the statue seemed almost human. She was wearing a long velvet cape, embroidered with gold designs, that was floor-length in the front and longer in the back. I was surprised to find that the doll I had created before even seeing her was an exact replica, right down to the red and gold cape which she only wears on her feast day. It was clear that I had connected with Our Lady of Health long before I arrived.

The morning of her feast day I awoke at 5:30 A.M. to the sound of bells from all of the town churches calling the faithful to Mass. When I arrived at the Basilica it was filled to capacity and I was one of a handful of Americans in the crowd. I wasn't able to understand the Spanish Mass so I went into a meditation of my own. The devotion and faith of the people were overwhelming as they crawled the length of the church in honor of their patron saint to reach the front altar for blessing. Midway through the service I felt energy pulsing through both of my hands, which I instinctively placed on my womb as I requested total healing. I received an inner message that I was to use my hands to do hands-on healing for others. I also knew I was to return home with my doll because she carried healing energy within her. I left Milagros with my request for healing when I went up to the statue of Our Lady of Health for her blessing. I saw what I can only describe as grace, in the form of tiny, twinkling starlight, falling from the sky onto the people present in the church. The sight of this brought me to tears. As the service ended 12-foot puppets of men and women came up the center isle and danced before Our Lady in a prayer of celebration and gratitude. It was so magical it took my breath away!

In the evening I went back for the healing service, which was attended by more than 3000 people filling the pews and aisles and spilling out all the doors. I was pulled into the church by the swelling crowd calling the Virgin from behind the curtain, using the Spanish words for "The Virgin Lives." As the chant grew louder the statue floated out from behind the curtain and 3000 people cheered. I stood in a sea of people as this beautiful Lady passed down the isle of the Basilica, appearing as though she were floating above us. I could see the tiny, twinkling stars of grace falling as if she were sprinkling us with blessings as she passed. When she came up the side aisle where I was standing she came within a foot of me. I was touched by the people as they lifted their small children so they could reach out to the hem of her long flowing cape as she passed by, in hopes that their child would receive a miracle. Witnessing this celebration made me feel certain that I too had experienced a miracle.

One is never the same when they return from a pilgrimage. It is important to set intentions carefully, for our words are very powerful. In asking for total healing I opened myself up to ten days where I had pain in every part of my body that had ever experienced trauma, because anything out of balance needed to be cleared. I deepened my connection to The Divine Feminine and felt cradled in the arms of Her Motherly love. I received healing on levels that I hadn't expected and can safely say I am not the same woman who committed to this pilgrimage. Despite the pain and numerous challenges I experienced in a land where I could not speak the language, the gifts I received made it all worth it. I know that the Divine lives in each one of us.

AWAKENING YOUR INNER PHYSICIAN

If you do decide to take a pilgrimage the preparation is as important as the journey. You want to find a place that immediately calls to you because that means there is something important there for you. You may not even have to leave home to do a pilgrimage and in some cases you might not even be able to leave home if you are too sick. After you choose where it is you want to go the preparation begins. There are many great books written both about pilgrimages and about the many sacred sites around the world. Reading might be the first step in your preparation.

There are times in all our lives when we need to step back, take time out and renew our inner spirit. That is the time for a pilgrimage. The inner pilgrimage is a beautiful journey to the heart of your own truth, the part of you that is awake, aware and connected to all that is. It is the sacred pilgrimage site that only you can access and it holds information that is just for you, that will help you on your journey to health and wellness.

You don't have to leave home to take a pilgrimage, since all pilgrimages are in reality inner pilgrimages. A pilgrimage is a sacred journey and the most sacred of journeys is the one within, so it doesn't matter where you go to experience one. You can also do a pilgrimage without leaving home if you can't fit an actual trip into your life.

You might want to explore places that appeal to you and create a pilgrimage around that. Find a place where you can create sacred space and put things there that represent the place as well as the issue you are working on. Dedicate a specific amount of time that you will spend in your sacred pilgrim space and go there every day for a week. You can journal, create intentional art or just meditate in that space to get answers that will support your healing.

The word "pilgrimage" derives from the Latin peregrinus, meaning "foreign," derived from peregre, meaning "going abroad," derived from "per-" (through) + "ager" (field). Therefore, a pilgrim is someone who is not at home. The inner pilgrimage is the journey taken to return home to your true self. When we are not home with our self or within our body disharmony occurs and out of disharmony comes disease. The inner pilgrimage is a journey to wholeness and health and self-transformation.

Your inner pilgrimage can be a daily, weekly, monthly or even yearly ritual. It can be as simple as finding a quiet space where you won't be disturbed, lighting a candle and meditating, or it can be as elaborate as you want it to be. Your inner pilgrimage can include journaling which is a great way to gain insight and perspective. If you are lucky enough to have a labyrinth near you, that can also be a form of inner pilgrimage. The point is that whatever you do, make it something that brings you into your center where you can connect with the wisdom of your Inner Physician. You can use my pilgrimage as a foundation for creating your own and if you keep reading you will find out how to make a healing doll and a medicine bag.

I have included a guided journey called "The Inner Pilgrimage" on the Empowered Health and Wellness: Awakening your Inner Physician CD, which is available at www.empoweredhealthandwellness.com.

CREATIVE TECHNIQUE FOR WELLNESS

Making a Doll for Well-being

"The use of Poppets (healing dolls) is an age old practice; the poppet itself is similar to a luck charm only much more powerful. Poppets can be used to promote health, healing, love, and happiness, to protect loved ones from harm, and to charm friends and enemies alike."

www.spiritual.com.au

Humans have always made creations in their own image: icons of Goddesses, then Gods, or playthings for children to learn and practice their places in their unique culture. Dolls are not just for girls or women but were made by shamans in some cultures. Throughout history man has used his own images, in the form of "dolls," to represent themselves as they approached the Gods in rituals and ceremonies to evoke healing.

The ancient Scots used dolls, called poppets, filled with herbs to aid in healing, to banish curses or protection against dark forces. Dolls or poppets were animated through intention and used in divination by Eskimo and the Javanese. In the ancient world dolls were usually made of rags, wood, paper, fruit, bone, wax, grains, and potatoes or fired clay. They ranged from simple homemade playthings to miniature works of art with finely worked features and jointed bodies. Some were filled with lavender and other herbs. The intention was that whatever actions were performed upon the effigy would be transferred to the subject based on sympathetic magic. A blessing or incantation was said over the doll and it was given to the individual to keep during the ritual for healing. Once the purpose was fulfilled the doll was buried to stop the spell.

The Incas and ancient Egyptians placed dolls in their burial chambers and tombs as guardians, guides or companions in the afterlife. American Indians used a type of doll in medicine ceremonies to bring healing energy to the sick.

Haitians and many African tribes use a type of talisman called Voodoo dolls for healing, fertility, gaining power, luck and placing curses on someone. When we think of Voodoo dolls they usually have a negative connotation, but originally the intention was for positive purposes.

The British Museum has a Roman rag doll, found in a child's grave dating back to 300 BC. Other early finds include 1st Century Peruvian dolls made from woven materials and 6th Century Coptic dolls made from brightly colored wool. They were not always used as toys, but as religious or fertility symbols. A fragment of an alabaster doll from the Babylonian period has been found. Dolls constructed of flat pieces of wood, painted with various designs and with "hair" made of strings of clay or wooden beads, have often been found in Egyptian graves dating back to 2000 BC. Egyptian tombs of wealthy families have included pottery dolls.

Native Americans have been making corn husk dolls for their children since they started raising corn for food. The brittle corn husks became soft and malleable after being soaked and they made a convenient and easily crafted toy. Besides giving the dolls to their children they were used in healing ceremonies. Dolls were usually made of perishable materials like corn husk, palmetto fiber, or bundled pine needles; even those that were made out of wood or leather were not meant to be permanent. A healing ceremony could be created and when complete the doll was thrown into a fire which was symbolic for letting go and releasing the problem to Great Spirit. To banish evil dreams the doll was buried in the earth and in this way the evil dream was carried away.

Kachina dolls are another Native American healing doll that represents spirits who live mostly in the San Francisco Hills in Flagstaff, Arizona. Kachinas originate from the religious and spiritual beliefs of the Pueblo Indians, in particular the Hopi and the Zuni and were gifts given in hope of future abundance and health, as well as tools for teaching children specific concepts. Kachinas are spirits, often of animals, who carry the prayers of the people. There are more than 250 different Kachinas, each with its own separate attributes, representing everything from animals to abstract concepts. A doll is crafted of cottonwood, painted and decorated with beads and feathers to represent the specific energy that was being called upon. The major concerns dealt with by Kachinas are rain, fertility, rich harvest, good health, long life, and to achieve balance and harmony in nature.

Shamans in Siberia created shaman dolls, called Nipopo Dolls ("wooden baby") which were wooden figurines, in the image of man, used symbolically for specific functions. Often in that tradition small dolls were also sewed on to their robes and used to represent the spirit world. Traditional shaman dolls represented the guardian, helper, and healer and were used as amulets for curing and warding off childhood disease. It was thought that by adding strips of red and blue cloth or blue beads the power was increased.

Some dolls were dressed in wood shavings to increase their efficacy. The general function of all of these dolls was to communicate to the spirit world. I imagine these primitive looking dolls were pretty powerful.

As you can see, dolls have been used for healing way back into history, but have been made less sacred by popularizing them as toys. If we look at their history it makes sense that they would still be used for that purpose today.

Healing dolls are created to address a specific area that a person desires to heal, which could be emotional, mental or spiritual. The personal intention of wellness is placed in the doll's inner body using stones, charms, hair from the person being healed, and other objects that represent the intention, like I did with my doll. The doll itself is a manifestation of that intention through color, fabric, beads, etc. The dolls I create are inspired by the Divine Feminine and Mother Mary. They are powerful tools for the intention of health because they carry the affirmation that one is already healed and whole.

When I created my doll I spent a lot of time deciding what to make her with, what fabric to use and what to put inside. I also wrote my intention on a piece of paper and placed it inside. Consequently she continues to carry the energy of healing and is a very powerful tool. The dolls give physical form to prayer. Whenever we pray for someone we are sending out our intent for that person's well-being. Dolls for well-being are physical manifestations of an intent for aiding someone or something. The idea of the healing doll is that it is a tangible symbol of a prayer and through its creation it is intended to give it form and bring about an awareness of the desire for health and wellness.

I described in a previous chapter the process I went through when I was diagnosed with a prolapsed womb and the doll I created for that purpose. I have found over the years that intention is strengthened by the creation of a visual object that acts as a symbol of the intention and that is why a doll is such a powerful tool. I created a powerful healing doll that I had intended to leave at the shrine, placing my hair, stones and other objects in her body. As I prepared to take the journey, I worked with the doll, through prayer and meditation, to strengthen my intention to heal. Inside the doll I placed stones, charms, my hair, a message on paper and some of my menstrual blood.

This doll accompanied me to over 50 churches in Mexico, including the national Shrine of Our Lady of Guadalupe. I was going to leave her at the shrine but my guidance told me to bring her home with me. She continues to hold the healing energy from all of the places I visited with her. When I feel I need any kind of healing I can hold the doll and connect with the healing energy of Mexico.

Wellness dolls can be simple or they can be elaborate, depending on your skills. The doll-making process is more important than how it looks. The intention behind them is what brings them alive and makes them a conduit for transformation. The intention is made more personal by the items you choose to put inside the body. The doll creates a visual link for you between your issue, the Divine, your Inner Physician and healing. If you decide to make a doll, put your heart and soul into it and it will become a powerful tool for healing.

AWAKENING YOUR INNER PHYSICIAN

A very simple doll can be made by taking two pieces of felt, cutting the shape of body, filling it with fiberfill, adding the objects you want to put into it and sewing around the edge about an 1/8th-1/4 of an inch in. Pick a color that feels healing to you. You can add hair using yarn. Make it small if you want a doll to carry with you or make it bigger if you want to place in on a special wellness altar you make specifically for that purpose. It is important not to worry about how the finished doll looks because creating it is a healing process which is more important than the completed project. For me the cruder and more primitive a doll looks the better. If you look at ancient healing dolls some of them are pretty funky and primitive and yet they feel very powerful. Some of the favorite dolls I have created are made from sticks that are wrapped and tied with fabric and decorated with feathers and beads.

You could make a corn husk doll like this: invoke the power of healing, place your illness in it and bury it in the ground in a ceremony to release disease. Imagine the disease being released and healed and the corn growing into a plant that will produce food. What an awesome metaphor for healing that would be!

I have made dolls by wrapping fiberfill, fabric and various charms and beads around a stick found outside. You can make a head out of clay if you want or make it by wrapping fabric. The tying of the fabric is what holds the doll together on the stick. As you wrap and tie you can state your intentions into the doll. These dolls are quick and easy to make so they can be burned if you choose.

Before you start your doll, go within and connect with your Inner Physician to ask for guidance. You can simply say, "What kind of doll is best for my purposes right now?" and see what comes. Jot down the information you receive and use this to help guide you in selecting your materials.

Things to put inside the doll's body:

- Stones: you can research the properties of stones to see what fits the best for your situation.

- A piece of your hair.

- A small note to your Inner Physician or the angel of your illness.

- Herbs: you can also do research for the herbs that are best for you.

- A charm that represents what you want as an outcome or a specific animal you feel connected to.

- A photo of yourself or someone who needs healing.

Energetically put the intention in the doll that the issue is already healed. Do this by holding the finished doll in your hands, closing your eyes and meditating on the intention with all of your heart. The doll is a link to your Inner Physician and each time you look at it or work with it you connect with your Higher Intelligence.

Now create an altar to focus on your healing journey. This will make your intention even stronger and more powerful. Find a table or dresser where you can create sacred space. Place things on the altar, including your doll, that represent wellness for you. Buy a special candle and some incense just for this altar.

Go to your sacred space whenever you need an extra boost and a positive healing focus.

If you don't have the skills to create your own doll you can ask a friend or family member to make one for you or commission one from an artist. To learn more about the healing dolls I create, e-mail me or go to www.empoweredhealthandwellness.com.

CREATIVE TECHNIQUE
FOR WELLNESS

Creating a Medicine Bag

"A well-tended medicine bag provides a stable foundation for your spiritual journey, catalyzing sustainable accelerated soul growth. Working with your medicine bag enables you to heal and transform with ever-increasing ease and clarity. As you work with your medicine bag, it progressively embodies and reflects the energies of your spirit and of the cosmos, becoming a powerful ally on your pathway to the luminous."

Ananaia O'Leary

I have made many medicine bags over the years. Some are small neck pieces that I wear and others are larger bags that I can carry. I made a special medicine bag in 2000 when I went on a pilgrimage to heal my womb. The bag carries an image of Guadalupe because I was working with her and intended to visit the National Shrine of Guadalupe in Mexico City. I placed items in the bag that would support my womb and healing it as well as objects that were given to me by friends for this purpose. Over the years since I created it I have taken it with me at other times to hold sacred space for me and I have added charms and stones to it.

I also have a special medicine bag that I made about 15 years ago to celebrate my solar return/birthday. The year for each of the celebrations is marked on the inside flap of the back as a record keeper. Inside are objects that are special to me. Over the years I have added something to the inside but every year on my birthday I add new charms to the bag by finding charms for the things I would like to manifest in the coming year and tying them on to ribbons. They are tied on to the flap of the bag, which is now heavy with charms and powerful with energy of every celebration.

The medicine bag is known in all cultures and throughout all of history. A medicine bag is an ancient item that spiritually represents the person who wears it or carries it. It creates a visual way to focus on something important. In 1991 the body of a man who lived over 5,000 years ago was found frozen in a high mountain range and with him was a medicine bag. Native people have carried medicine bags for hundreds of years as a way of protecting objects that are sacred to them and important in their healing work. Traditionally most Native American men carried a "medicine bag," or "bundle" as it is called with the intention of bringing protection, good luck, and carrying the energy of healing. It is created as a vessel, or temple space for your sacred objects. The bag can be made of leather and decorated with beads, charms and symbols that are specific to your path and soul purpose at this time. It can also contain objects such as leaves, feathers, stones, herbs such as sweet grass, sage, cedar, lavender or pinon, and other objects which have been added by the wearer and considered spiritually significant. South American medicine men and women create what they call a mesa, which carries all of their sacred objects. It is a bundle that is opened during ceremony and spread out on the cloth that makes up the carrying vessel. The reasons to carry a medicine bag are for guidance, healing and protection.

A medicine bag can be small to hang around your neck or three or four feet long containing objects and substances which have meaning to the owner. Often they were made from the skin of an animal and usually that of an unborn buffalo calf. Most medicine bags throughout history contained a clear quartz crystal. They were readily available and this is a stone that most shamans feel is the most powerful to use. The quartz is usually referred to as "living rock" because it has memory and can be programmed. Objects kept in the bag are referred to as power objects and all are considered sacred. Power objects both personal and spiritual could be real or symbolic. It is believed that herbs, roots and stones could have real powers to make its owner physically well again. Sage, sweet grass and calamus root are common herbs found in medicine bags. Some objects placed in the medicine bag had deep spiritual significance to the person such as mementos from events, vision quests or pilgrimages.

The word totem animal refers to an animal that a person is closely identified with and feels a kinship for, as I do the swan and the hummingbird. You can put something to represent the power of your personal animal in your medicine bag. For example, if a shaman found a swan's feather (the swan being the bird that symbolizes Yogasete, the creator) it could acquire an air of magic and go into the bag.

The shaman carries a medicine bag that has items in it for healing him- or herself and others. Medicine bags are considered living things and honored as such. Many people believe that the medicine bag is a holy and sacred item and should never be opened by anyone aside from its owner. It contains personal holy items which are infused with the owner's energy which shouldn't be disrupted by someone else's energy so it is best not to have other people handle your sacred objects. I think this is a matter of personal choice and a respect for boundaries. I always ask someone before I touch items of spiritual importance to them.

Carrying a medicine bag will increase your awareness of your own sacredness. As you go through life you may find other things you want to add to your medicine bag. If you wear it and add to it throughout the years it becomes a spiritual scrapbook of your life, your travels, your achievements, and who you really are and is a wonderful thing to hand down to grandchildren who can understand its meaning and respect its value as you now do.

Some people create one medicine bag and it becomes the tool for focusing, or you can create a specific medicine bag for a specific purpose, as I have done. You could create a medicine bag that represents health and wellness so that it is a reminder of the state of health you want to be in. To make your medicine bag, you can purchase a leather pouch or make your own from a piece of hide or natural colored canvas. You can decorate the outside of your bag with symbols or drawings that are significant to you and what you want to focus on. I add charms, beads and other decorations to the outside.

Add items that will remind you of the intention you are focusing on and place it somewhere that it can be seen every day to help you hold the intention.

AWAKENING YOUR INNER PHYSICIAN

Medicine bags can be as small as 1 inch by 1 inch or as large as 30 inches in length. They are typically made of leather and you can purchase such a bag to make your own at most metaphysical stores. The outside of your bag should be a natural color or earth tone like tan. Most medicine bags contain a quartz crystal as one of its objects. Quartz energy resonates with all the energies of the physical body and is considered a remarkable healing stone. It connects you to your spiritual self. You can decorate the outside of your bag with symbols or drawings of animals or leaves, whatever feels right in your heart.

Other items you might like in your own medicine bag are items you may have found a special attraction to or resonance with in your life. For example, a special shell you found at the seashore or a feather you found or a piece of pine tree or a juniper berry all can hold meaning for you. We often meet up with items that seem to be just waiting for us to pick them up and carry them home and then we don't know what to do with them. This is one place to give them a home close to your heart. The essence of these special items creates an energy in your medicine bag and that energy is the force that represents you. So by creating a medicine bag and wearing it close to your heart you are connecting with your spiritual self, the authentic you and always remembering who you are.

Here is a very simple medicine bag you can make yourself.

1. Cut a 6 inch circle out of leather and punch an odd number of uniformly spaced holes about 1/2" from the edge of the leather. Thirteen holes should be enough. You can make the circle bigger if you want but you will need more holes.

2. Decorate the bag with symbols that you feel connected with if you want.

3. Begin by putting the lacing which is at least 18 inches long into one of the holes from the outside (or smooth) side of the leather. Weave the leather lacing in and out of the remaining holes all around the circle.

4. Push the lacing out through the first hole. There should be two pieces of lacing going through this hole.

5. Push in the middle of the circle and pull on both ends of the leather lacing to form the pouch.

6. Add beads, feathers, or a stopper knot to the lacing if desired.

The bag needs to be empowered at this point, which means infusing it with your energy, and filled with sacred objects. Before placing your items in your bag take a moment to bless them; think of why each object is important to you and why you want to put it in your medicine bag. Bless Mother Earth and her creatures for providing these things for you. Lay all the objects you wish to put in your bag and the bag itself on a table. You can create sacred space to do this empowerment ritual, simply by lighting a candle and burning some incense. Hold each object in your hand, close your eyes, and think about what you would like it to do. Run it through the smoke from the incense to cleanse it and put it inside the bag. Do this for each item, one at a time.

Think of how carrying this medicine bag represents your connection to your spiritual nature and your own power to heal and to guide and protect others. Carrying the medicine bag will increase your awareness of your own sacredness and the bag becomes empowered and imbued with your healing energy. If you wear it and add to it throughout the years it becomes a spiritual representation of your life, your travels and your achievements along your spiritual path. After you have put all your sacred things into the bag hold it in your hand and meditate on what you want to do with it and how it can assist you in your healing. Thank all of the objects for being of assistance to you.

CHAPTER SEVEN

Dreaming your way to Wellness

"A Healing Dream can never be completely 'interpreted,' or fully understood. Healing Dreams want us to stop making sense; not just to crack the case, but to enter the mystery."

Marc Ian Barasch, Healing Dreams

One of the ways our Inner Physician communicates with us is through our dreams. We can ask questions of our dreams and get answers. More often information just comes through the dream which helps us see an issue that we might not have been aware of. To illustrate once more the power of the body to return to balance I want to share an experience that blows my mind even today. For several weeks at the end of 2004 I had experienced severe pain in my abdomen sometimes two or three times a day. I became concerned that it might be a problem with my gallbladder so I went to the doctor. The doctor sent me to the hospital to have an ultrasound and I was diagnosed with severe gallbladder disease, with fibroids in the gallbladder which needed surgical removal. The doctor told me that the only thing that could be done was to remove the diseased gallbladder.

My past experience with my body gave me courage to tell my doctor I wouldn't have the surgery and that I would work with alternative methods. She smiled her skeptical smile and agreed to forgo surgery, reminding me that I could call when I was ready to do it. I feel that the gallbladder was put in the body for a reason and it has an important function. I didn't want to disturb the homeostasis by having it removed if I didn't have to. I know a lot of people have their gallbladders removed and live perfectly normal lives but I didn't want to use that option. I trust my body and felt it could resolve itself and I was willing to endure some pain to explore the possibility.

Several times a month I would have problems with my gallbladder after eating. In May 2005 I began to have daily problems that got so severe that I was considering having it removed. The pain worsened and began to occur three or four times a day, lasting for several hours making me very uncomfortable. One of the biggest challenges was trying not to focus on the pain and to visualize my gallbladder as well and healthy. I learned from the past that the more I focused on pain the more the physical problem increased. What we think about increases according to the law of attraction. It is very difficult when you are experiencing physical pain to take your focus off of it, but it is necessary if you want to effect healing.

One day I was talking to my daughter who was getting very concerned about me.

She encouraged me to go back to the doctor and have the surgery. I told her that if I didn't feel better in a few days I promised I would have my gallbladder taken out. At that point the pain was more than I wanted to deal with much longer and it was beginning to look like the best option.

Here are the excerpts from my journal at the time, where I talk about using Radiant Frequencies, a system I created that you will learn about later:

May 23, 2005: Severe gallbladder attack. I am working with gallbladder, liver, and elimination Radiant Frequencies for the first time. I had an almost immediate response using the gallbladder frequency card and drumming over my gallbladder with my healing Kultrun drum. Later in the day I was pain free for the first time in a couple of weeks.

During the session I went inside my gallbladder visually and watched as the fibroids liquefied and flushed out of my gallbladder. I feel I need to work more with this visualization, as I was able to see four of them dissolve and I feel there are more.

As you can see from that entry I am using a combination of visualization, sound healing and Radiant Frequencies which is an energy system, to support my healing process and it is showing results.

May 25th, 2005: I had another attack which was milder than the one before. I used the Gallbladder Radiant Frequencies card and drum and the pain stopped within 20 minutes.

May 28th, 2005: Since I began using Radiant Frequencies (see following chapter for more about Radiant Frequencies) I have been moving through fear of having surgery and have moved to acceptance. I feel that the Frequencies have brought up the fear for me so I could explore where it was coming from and release it. This morning I had a dream that I had surgery and the doctor had my gallbladder removed too. The doctor was actually a couple of large, angelic beings. The surgery was today (5-28) in the dream but I knew in the dream that it took place on May 29th. I remember how good I felt in the dream and how I reached down to touch under my rib cage and could feel the stitches where the gallbladder was removed. In the early stages of waking from the dream I realized that I had lived through the surgery. One of the fears I had been having was that I would die on the operating table. The dream was telling me that I survived the surgery and this seemed like a prophetic message. It made it easier for me to decide that I would be willing to have surgery if I didn't feel better in a few days.

That was May 28, 2005 and I still have my gallbladder and it is problem free ~ it is 9 years later and I have had no problems with my gallbladder. I believe that miracles can happen in all kinds of ways so why not through a dream? Sometimes I wonder if my gallbladder was removed through some etheric surgery or if I was given a new one or if my old one was repaired while I was dreaming. There is no way that I could have had a diseased gallbladder and then not have a diseased gallbladder unless a miracle had occurred. When I went for my physical the next year I told the doctor I no longer had problems with my gallbladder. She just shook her head and had nothing to say. I couldn't tell her that some dream doctors took care of the problem; I kept that to myself.

An important component to the shift was the fact that I let go and accepted what was happening. I came into alignment and acceptance with my body and its wisdom. I accepted the fact that my physical intelligence might have its own reason for wanting to release my gallbladder from my body. Until we can let go, we are holding our body to a particular destiny because we are focusing on the disorder of our body. Once we let go, healing can begin because we have moved into a space of harmony with our body. We are in harmony because we are no longer fighting. When I stopped fighting with my body and being upset for the condition that I was experiencing, my Inner Physician and angels could step into the space and do what they needed to do. The act of letting go is not giving up, it is releasing our grip so there is space for something to happen. This is the space where miracles can occur.

I continued to work with Radiant Frequencies and received deeper information about how to use them. It is clear to me that they are to be used with sound such as drums, rattles and chanting so I am preparing to learn more about healing with sound. I believe that Radiant Frequencies assisted me in restoring my gallbladder.

CREATIVE TECHNIQUE FOR WELLNESS

Radiant Frequencies

"I believe that symbolic language is the one foreign language that each of us must learn."

Erich Fromm, Forgotten Language

Radiant Frequencies is a healing tool that uses symbol and color to impact the different systems of the body. It was gifted to me and named through a spiritual connection with the Egyptian master, Thoth, on the lunar eclipse on April 24th, 2005. It came to me like a flash of lightning, and without a break 40 symbols came to me over a period of an hour as I sat in a hotel room in Burlington, Vermont.

I was in the final phase of my trip to Vermont for my artist fellowship, staying in Burlington, Vermont for the weekend, when Radiant Frequencies was presented to me. I am very familiar with the quality of the spiritual connection through which this came because it is the same way all of my visionary art comes and the way my children's game came to me in 1996. I had just come from a total immersion experience with the energy of Venus. I had created that space so I could paint images that were connected to Venus and swans. The space I created connected me very deeply to Egypt, so it was little surprise to me that this would come from the Egyptian God Thoth. I had gotten up that morning and took a bus downtown and hadn't been there long when something told me to go back to my hotel. When I arrived at my room I suddenly got very sick as though I had the intestinal flu and it remained with me until all the symbols and their colors were given and the process was complete and then I spontaneously felt better.

At first I was surprised and excited about the possibilities but the more I thought about what had happened the more my resistance grew. I can be as skeptical as anyone when it comes to the non-tangible. I began to think the same things the others might think of such a thing, such as, "How do I know this will heal people?" "Why would it come to me?" "Thoth, are you crazy?" "Who do I think I am?" I imagine many people who are either giving or receiving healing question if and how healing happens. Visionaries frequently question their visions because of where they come from and I am no exception.

When I returned home I did research to find out why this information would come to me through Thoth, thinking it would alleviate my resistance. I wasn't convinced that Radiant Frequencies could work. I didn't feel comfortable telling anyone about it and actually felt a little embarrassed when I did. I have only shared this with a few close friends and some clients until right now. I realize part of my resistance to sharing this information comes from my psychotherapy training over the years. I was trained that it is best to experience firsthand any technique you want to use on clients before you offer it to others. This belief comes from age-old wisdom that says you cannot safely guide another where you haven't gone yourself. I needed firsthand experience that this system works in order to feel comfortable.

Before I write more about Radiant Frequencies let me share what the research said about Thoth. I learned that Thoth, one of the Ascended Masters and a God in Egyptian mythology, was an ancient healer who used light, color, sound and symbol. He worked with the Language of Light, creating pictures and hieroglyphs that were healing and transformative. The Ascended Masters are connecting with and blessing many healers at this time, with ancient wisdom regarding healing and balance, to assist in our current evolution on Earth. Thoth is often referred to as the original author of the Hermetic texts, a collection of magical works said to contain all the mystical knowledge of the ancient world. He revealed to mankind the healing arts, mystical wisdom, magic, art, hieroglyphics and astronomy.

The caduceus carried by Thoth is used as the modern symbol for medicine. The caduceus represents the DNA helix, shown as two intertwined snakes, and it contains the crystalline frequency of all morphogenetic fields, which connect all living beings through the Language of Light.

Thoth believes that healing is very simple and we make it more complicated when we get stuck in our fear. In a state of fear our mind creates all kinds of stories about what is happening to us. Radiant Frequencies uses the Language of Light and symbolic image, color and vibration as the vehicle for healing and each key/image is encoded with a healing mantra. It is simple to use yet very powerful in its ability to heal. The Language of Light is our seed language created at the beginning of time and recorded in our DNA. When we work with it we understand it at a soul level. It is the word made flesh from which all of creation was born.

The foundation of language and writing is purely symbolic. The Language of Light courses through our nervous system. Encoding the natural waveform geometry of the physical world, the Language of Light is a harmonic language, which mimics the waveform properties of light. Given the research it is clear that Radiant Frequencies are very connected with Thoth.

What does this mean on a practical level as far as maintaining or returning to wellness is concerned? The principles discovered in Dr.Masaru Emoto's water research are also supportive of the healing powers of Radiant Frequencies. The body is made mainly of water and Dr. Emoto discovered that water has the ability to take the images in and utilize them for healing and restructuring. Holding the card in the hand informs the cells through the water in our bodies. I was surprised the first time I held one of the cards as I felt tingling in my hands and warmth throughout my body.

Radiant Frequencies work with the person to restore harmony and balance to the body. As you experience the energy of Radiant Frequencies anything that is not in alignment with harmony will come up for release, such as past and present life issues that are stored in the cells of the body. The process is intended as a gentle release and that which you need to see and experience in order to evolve will be shown to you in a gentle manner and then it is released.

Radiant Frequencies are 2-inch x 2-inch cards that fit into the palm of the hand. Each symbol has a specific color combination. Each has a special mantra that is said to activate it, and once activated it stays activated. I activated all 44 cards one night and it put me into an altered healing space that was very powerful. The cards were placed in a window in the moonlight from the new moon to the full moon to set the mantras of intention and expose them to the balancing power of sun and moon light.

I feel blessed to have been the vehicle for such a powerful tool for bringing balance and wellness into the body. I have experienced a number of healings using Radiant Frequencies and so have my clients. Our natural state is that of health and wellness and we are being supported to find ways to bring that balance into our bodies. Radiant Frequencies is one of the tools to assist us in doing that.

AWAKENING YOUR INNER PHYSICIAN

You might choose to discover your own symbol set to work with. Find a quiet place where you won't be disturbed for 30 minutes to an hour. Quiet yourself and go within. When you feel that your mind is quiet ask your Inner Physician to send you a set of symbols that you can use to help you heal your current issue. Listen quietly and trust what you hear. You may only get one symbol or you might get several. Try to draw them the best you can. When you are complete, thank your Inner Physician. Either draw your symbol or see if you can find a picture of it and begin to work with it each day for a few minutes. Your personal symbols are very powerful healing agents.

You can order a set of Radiant Frequencies Cards at www.empoweredhealthandwellness.com.

See the information at the back of the book.

CHAPTER EIGHT

Eyes are the Window to the Soul

"My eyes are an ocean in which my dreams are reflected."

"There is a road from the eye to heart that does not go through the intellect."

G. K. Chesterton

You would think by this time I would have learned all of my lessons from my body and that I would not have to learn that way anymore. That is what I thought too, but apparently not. You might be thinking that after all I have been through I shouldn't have to have one more thing. I have always made some of the deepest transformation in my evolution though issues with my body. Unfortunately I still had something to learn from my wise Inner Physician, that I could apparently only learn through my body. I feel that if you end up with an issue with your health and body you have something important to learn.

In July 2006 I went to a group experience in which the person was working with

"The Spirit Doctors," who are said to be a group of doctors working in another realm. I went because a friend had invited me to go, not because I thought I had something that needed to be healed. During the session I had the awareness that my eyes were the focus of the work. The next morning I woke with a light flashing in my left eye. This flashing went on for about an hour and then my left eye filled with floating debris. For the first couple weeks my vision was greatly hindered by all of the debris. During the day I could see all of the particles floating around in my eye and it was extremely distracting. It helped to wear sunglasses at all times. At night, driving was nearly impossible. Although it was in my left eye both of my eyes were impacted because they focus together.

Having a problem with my vision was frightening for me, as I suspect it would be for many people. Without sight we live in a different world and because I am such a visual person, an artist and a writer it was very distressing to me to have this problem. I couldn't imagine living the rest of my life with my vision clouded by debris. I was angry at myself for going to this healing in the first place and at the woman who facilitated it, for not knowing what she was doing and for screwing up my eyes with her stupid "Spirit Doctors."

After two weeks and no improvement I decided I needed to see a doctor. My primary care physician referred me the eye doctor. The appointment with the eye doctor was very intense. She performed a number of tests which required my eye to be numbed and dilated. As I waited for my eyes to dilate my vision grew more blurry. It had been a long time since I had my eyes dilated and I had forgotten this is what happens. As my vision deteriorated I had thoughts of what it would mean to me if I lost my sight. Here I was, alone in the waiting room and my vision was disappearing and I had to drive myself home after the exam. I sat in terror waiting for the doctor to return.

At the end of the exam the eye doctor told me in a matter of fact way that I had a Posterior Vitreous Detachment, PVD in my left eye. She also said that the debris in my eye was permanent. Here I was again in the presence of a woman doctor with an attitude that it was no big deal. She had a poor bedside manner and it was a big deal to me. I still haven't figured out why I have drawn so many doctors without compassion to me. I left the doctor's office wearing the geeky sunglasses they gave me and went to my car where I sat and cried. After a few minutes of grief I sat up in my seat and said out loud "Nothing is Permanent!" At that point my resolve to heal kicked in.

That same day a new Radiant Frequencies symbol came to me to use for balancing the eye. I drew the symbol and began working with it. A few days later I was at the bookstore and a book on sacred geometry caught my eye. As I looked through it I saw my new Radiant Frequencies symbol for the eye on the page and it was said to be a symbol for the eye. I was shocked and surprised for a moment and that was followed by that knowing smile that I had tapped into something high that is connected to all wisdom and that is why I was able to draw the exact symbol for the eye, even though I hadn't seen it before. I don't know why it always surprises me when I get intuitive information through my art that is so accurate but it does.

As I worked with the symbol I began to receive information about the Eye of Horus and a connection to my eye. My guidance lead me to a very specific store that I had only been to one other time and where I was told by my Inner Physician that I would find a lapis Eye of Horus that I could use in my healing. I went to the store looking for the lapis Eye of Horus but found nothing. Someone came into the store behind me and said, "Where is all of your jewelry?" to which the owner said, "I haven't put it out yet." She put jewelry on the bottom shelf of the case and when she was done she took two lapis Eyes of Horus out of a box and placed them on the top shelf. When you start to experience synchronicity like this, know that you are being guided by something higher because there isn't any earthly explanation.

Once again I was stunned by my inner guidance yet glad I had listened to it. I learned that the eyes were carved by a street vendor in Egypt and were a one-of- a-kind set. I bought the set and took them home and began to work with them and the Radiant Frequencies. For me it is more powerful if I have a physical representation of the metaphor that I am working with. Not only did I have a physical representation of the metaphor, but also it came in the healing stone of lapis.

The Eye of Horus is said to be filled with specific minerals and plants. It was used whenever the balance and order of nature had been disrupted, which disease is, or an assailing foe needed to be defended against, such as an immunity-response. The Eye of Horus had revitalizing abilities. The Egyptians used both eyes in various ways stressing their complements as sun and moon or masculine and feminine. Since I was working on balancing the masculine and feminine inside me at the time this seemed fitting.

One night I woke up from sleep and my eyes were so full of floating things that I could barely see. I was also seeing large black spots and flashing lights. I was concerned that they were getting worse. As I lay in my bed in fear I got the idea that I should put my hands over my eyes and send energy to them. I rubbed my hands together and placed them both over my left eye. When I removed them a couple of minutes later the eye was clear. I rubbed my hands together again and placed them on my right eye. It cleared a bit but it would take a few more hours to completely clear.

Today my eyes are clear unless I am tired or under stress when they will get a little blurry. Once again I followed the seemingly strange advice of my Inner Physician and my body got just what it needed so it could come back into well-being.

Let's explore a bit more about using metaphors for healing.

CREATIVE TECHNIQUE
FOR WELLNESS

Metaphors for Wellbeing

"The power of metaphorical interventions may lie in the fact that metaphorical images are distributed throughout the brain in a holographic manner. If so, then exploring linguistic metaphors and early memory metaphors may activate this expansive network, and transforming metaphors may reverberate throughout the entire range of distribution of the image and/or memory."

Richard R. Kopp, Metaphor Therapy, Brunner/Mazell, New York, 1995

Metaphors are one of the most powerful change techniques available in my experience. Metaphor is one way the soul and the Inner Physician speak to us and when we begin to discover our personal symbols/metaphors we can take our healing and transformation to a new level.

Our words, thoughts, and feelings are vibrantly alive and have an impact on our bodies. All of our thoughts and memories, emotions, injuries, experiences and ancestry are stored in the muscles, tissues, cells and bones. We literally "embody" everything we have experienced, which is stored in our cells, through the mind-body connection. We are infinitely complex, multidimensional beings with vast amounts of data genetically encoded in our cells. Ordinary language is saturated with body metaphors. We frequently speak of "the lip of a cup, "and "the legs of a table, " and use expressions like "the walls have ears," "the interviewer kept me on my toes" and "let's get to the heart of the matter." Many of our metaphorical expressions are rooted in the body and our experiences of it, and metaphors, significantly shape our cultural perceptions of the body. It is giving us information all of the time and metaphor is a way to tap into that information.

The word metaphor comes from the Greek word "metaphora" which means "transference" and it has generally been understood as a figurative expression that makes an implied comparison with something else. Comparisons that use metaphors show how two things that are not very much alike are similar in one important way. It is the similarity between them that is the clue to the deeper issue that needs exploration.

People often use metaphor spontaneously in conversation to describe their symptoms. We can use these metaphors to activate a health-creating process and shift the mind to a new perspective because they play with language in unusual ways. This playful attitude bypasses the seriousness of the mind and allows something to happen. Here are a couple of examples of metaphors that can become issues in the body: "He is a pain in the neck," or "You are a pain in the butt!" We all know what those phrases mean when we hear them. I say, be careful what you say!

We can communicate with each part of our body, and discover the issues and blockages and heal them. One way to do this is to play in the metaphor of what is happening in your body. When I was working with my uterus I went to a quiet place in me and asked questions about what was happening and what my uterus needed. I simply tuned into my uterus and with paper and pencil began having a dialogue. It sounds silly but I got new information that I could work with, which helped in my healing process. Louise Hay has 2 books, called "Heal Your Body" and "You Can Heal Your Life" and in them she talks about body issues as metaphor. She addresses the problems of each body part in alphabetical order, giving each a mental cause and then a healing affirmation. She begins with an explanation of how every thought we think affects our body and how all the old negative thoughts we have harbored about ourselves have combined to send us a wake-up call.

Negative and positive emotions accumulated over a lifetime are stored not only in the mind as memories but also in the body and can become an integral part of our personality and identity. Since many of the memories are unconscious and don't represent our true nature they can block success in a variety of areas in life. You can enter your body through your intuitive, active imagination and engage it in a dialogue that can lead to an image or metaphor that shows you how to remedy the situation. Often one metaphor leads to another, taking you deep into your cellular memory. Focusing directly on the metaphors can create change on all levels. It is also a way of bypassing conscious roadblocks and engaging the creativity of the unconscious mind.

Many people can get caught in the intensity of negative emotion and get stuck. It is natural to begin to connect an emotion with a negative event in the past but this will also draw you deeper into the past and away from resolution. Creating a metaphor for the emotion or physical pain keeps you present and moves you forward and out of the pain.

I want to share my process as a way of illustrating how to use metaphor for transformation, sharing the symbols, history and meaning and how I worked with the information. During my years of self-healing I have found that using metaphor has taken me deeper into my healing process and lead to transformation. Through metaphor I have been able to come to the core of a problem and when it is transformed the physical problem clears up. When I experienced the detachment in my eye I worked with the metaphor of the Eye of Horus as well as other metaphors about the eye. Martin Brofman says, "Vision is a metaphor for the way we see the world and is related to personality." Once the elements of a person's experience that relate to their impaired vision are identified and released, then clear vision can be restored. Stress is responsible for all emotional and physical imbalances, and stress reflects how an individual interacts with his or her environment in a way which is not "at ease."

The physical eye is where we perceive light and information, but to the Egyptians, it is a symbol for spiritual energies and abilities. The Egyptian symbol is also known as the Udjat or Wedjat eye. The right eye is called the eye of Ra, and the left eye is called the Eye of Thoth and together they are known as the eyes of Horus, the Elder.

The name wedjat means "the sound eye" or "the sound one," "the magical healing eye" used for bringing things back into order after some kind of disturbance. The Eye of Horus refers to the lunar left eye of Horus that was plucked out by his rival Set during their conflict over the throne. The restoration of the eye is attributed to Thoth, Lord of Wisdom and Healing. The eye was healed and returned to Horus on the sixth lunar day. Horus used the first wedjat eye as an amulet that he offered to Osiris. It was so powerful that it restored him to life. The regenerative and protective powers of the amulet of the Eye of Horus made it the most popular of Egyptian amulets.

The Right Eye of Horus represents concrete factual information controlled by the left brain. It deals with words, letters, numbers and those things which are described in terms of sentences or complete thoughts. It approaches the Universe in terms of male-oriented ideation. It is a symbol of the sun.

The Left Eye of Horus represents abstract aesthetic information controlled by the right brain. It deals with esoteric thoughts and feelings and is responsible for intuition. It approaches the Universe in terms of female oriented ideation. We use the Left Eye, female-oriented, right side of our brain for feeling and intuition. It is a symbol of the moon. Together they create a whole and balanced perspective.

Working with the metaphor of the Eye of Horus it became clear to me that the issue with my eye was about my ability to trust the feminine and my ability to manifest and receive what I desire, even though there is no physical evidence in my world to support what I am visualizing. Here I was experiencing deep levels of the rejection of the feminine again. The doctor had told me I was right eye dominant which suggested that I needed to bring my left eye into a more balanced place so neither dominated. It is interesting that the problem I am having is with my left eye because that is the Eye of Horus that was injured and subsequently healed.

The next day I got another metaphor that rang true: "My detachment is causing a lack of clarity in my vision." Not only was the vision in my physical eye full of debris but all I could see on my path to manifesting my dreams was obstacles. I had the sense that because it has taken so long and I wasn't seeing evidence in my world I had become detached from my vision. I had taken on a "Whatever" attitude and that is what the Universe reflected back to me. Nothing can manifest in that environment.

I began to work with a new affirmation: "My vision is clear and focused and I see clearly that my dreams are manifesting in my life now." With this affirmation came more things that needed to be released. As I continued to work with metaphors about my vision, the debris in my eye began to disappear. I became aware of how important my eyes are to my creative process and how they help me write. When they are blurry I have a hard time staying focused and seeing what I need to edit or move. When they are clear it is easy to see how things should fit together. As I wrote this chapter I noticed all the words I used that are related to the eye, such as, focus, seeing, "caught my eye" and how it is such an important part of who I am. As I resolved the issues shown to me through the metaphors my vision cleared up.

I have worked with metaphor many times in my transformational process and have found it to be a catalyst for powerful change. I hope this helps give you an idea of how to use metaphor to heal and transform your physical health. You can also use metaphor to heal and transform emotionally and spiritually. As you work with metaphor you can use the words that come up in the process to go deeper. Personally I find that I have issues with my body when the Universe has tried all other avenues to get my attention. When I can discover the metaphor and work with it what was once hidden is brought into view and my body can release the issue so I can transform.

AWAKENING YOUR INNER PHYSICIAN

Let's explore the metaphors you might be having as a result of your current health concern. Look back at how I used metaphor to discover what my issues where and what they were trying to say to me.

What is Metaphor? There is a link between the mind and the symptoms and illnesses that turn up in our bodies. The link that psychology uses to examine the body through the mind is metaphor. Metaphor works because we are storytelling creatures and everything in our lives is part of our story. We learn about metaphor very early in life because it is used in advertising and in fairy tales.

Our mind is telling a specific story through our physical symptoms. Our mind interprets the type of symptom that we have, describes the physiological dynamic that is going on and all of this has a certain meaning to us. When we explore the metaphor our body is using we can find out what the story is that the mind is trying to tell us. It can be fun to explore the story and, like a detective, discover the meaning.

When you first start playing with metaphor you might need the help of a therapist or you can do research on your own. Once you discover the meaning you can use it like a map to help you heal the physical issue. When you clear out the emotional and psychological issues behind the metaphor the physical issue can clear too.

Here is a link to a web site that has many body metaphors for you to study:

http://www.healingkeys.com/MetaphorAtoZ.htm
(www.healingkeys.com).

Here is an example from the web site about the gallbladder to give you an idea about using the body metaphor:

"The gall bladder is a pear-shaped sac on the under-surface of the right lobe of the liver. Part of its function is to provide gastric juices to the digestive process to help break food down for assimilation. Problems with the gall bladder indicate that feelings of anger and bitterness have become overwhelming and that we are judging what is going on. We feel attacked and bitter about something and/or someone's bold effrontery (gall). We are projecting arrogance from a shadow figure, a part of ourselves that we have fractured off as an unbearable belief about our self."
Janie Ticehurst

CHAPTER NINE

A "Lightening" Bolt to the Side of the Head!

Human life is as evanescent as the morning dew or a flash of lightning. "

Samuel Butler

"Sometimes pain was like a storm that came out of nowhere. The clearest summer morning could end in a downpour. Could end in lightning & thunder."

Benjamin Alire Sáenz

I find it was interesting that I misspelled the word lightning in the title using the word lightening instead. Lightening was the end result and for that reason I left it as it is.

I took the leap of faith and quit my job as a psychologist! My career spanned 26 years and it was part of my identity. I have wanted to do it for a long time because I had a long list of other things I wanted to pursue. It was time to do what I came here to do, which includes painting, writing, inspiring people to live their best lives and encouraging others to follow their dreams. The day my departure was announced at the clinic where I was working I was struck with the worst headache I have ever had. It was like being struck by lightning on the left side of my face, with pulses of electrical current surging through my face every few minutes. I tried everything to make it go away but it wouldn't budge!

I was worried about how my leaving the clinic would affect the clients I was working with because some of them depended on our weekly sessions to stay grounded and one in particular had a lot of issues around being abandoned. I dreading having to tell each of them I would no longer be doing therapy.

By the third day I got the strongest headache medicine I could get over the counter and for 5 hours the headache was gone. It was my birthday and I wasn't going to let a headache spoil a day I had planned for two months. I had a great time at the party and made a lot of memories. The next morning I woke up with welts all over the left side of my face, on my forehead and across my eyelid and that was the beginning of my journey with shingles.

Shingles, isn't that something that they put on the roof to keep rain from getting in? Yes and no.

Shingles is a stupid word for a very painful condition! For me it included electrical shocks to the side of my head, across my forehead and into my eyelid, nausea, headache for days, numbness and a bug crawling feeling, no appetite and zero energy. I basically felt terrible for 2 weeks, spent most of the time horizontal eating very little. I couldn't sleep so I felt exhausted at a deep level. I started seeing dust and dirt in my house that I hadn't noticed before and I wanted it all to go away, but I didn't have energy to do anything about it.

Apparently shingles is a resurgence of the dormant chicken pox virus, which lurks silently in your nerves for years, until a moment of high stress triggers an ambush to knife you while you're already down. The funny thing is, I didn't feel stressed, but somewhere in my psyche I must have been. There was a part of my unconscious that has been split open by this bolt of lightning and it manifested though my dreams. A week into my journey with shingles I started to have dreams. The first series of dreams was about men from my past. Each night featured a different man and the illumination of the problem in our relationship. I saw each relationship from a vantage point I hadn't seen before. A theme emerged and I knew upon waking that I would not repeat the issue ever again. I also had a series of dreams about my work as a therapist, and how good I am at that. I see this as a graceful closure to a career I dedicated 26 years to.

The next series of dreams went so deep that I couldn't remember them when I woke up but knew that something had been changed in me through the night's journey. I believe our bodies tell us things we can't see another way, so I like to explore what the metaphor of a specific illness might be. Louise Hay says that shingles is about trust and the mantra she attaches to it is, "I am relaxed and peaceful because I trust the process of life and all is well in my world." Easy for you to say, Louise! I just quit a job that has been safe and created my stability for 25 years. Trust! Yeah, right, here I am leaping off the cliff and immediately I come down with some medical issue that costs over $600 because I don't have insurance. Now there is a trust building activity for you!

I had tried this retirement thing two times before and ended up going back to safety and stability after hitting bottom. The last two times I quit my job to follow my dreams I was in a different consciousness. I live in abundance consciousness now so I don't have to worry about not having support or having my needs met. I always have what I need. This time would be different because I had a plan in place to replace my income but it was still frightening to quit a long career that was fulfilling.

Having shingles is an enormous lesson in patience as there is no way of speeding up the healing process and your energy comes back when it wants to, not when you want it to. When I looked up the metaphysical meaning of shingles I found numerous references that it was the sign of a spiritual awakening. I can buy that. It did feel like something had broken through the side of my face and the rash seemed like the perfect sign that something was being released.

This was a spiritual awakening about trust, an issue I have often struggled with. On the deepest level it is about trusting myself to know that I can leap into my dreams, follow my heart and be relaxed and peaceful in the process, because all is very well with my world.

CREATIVE TECHNIQUE
FOR WELLNESS

Imagery and Imagination for Wellness

"The spirit is the master, imagination the tool, and the body the plastic material.

The power of the imagination is a great factor in medicine. It may produce diseases…and it may cure them. Ills of the body may be cured by physical remedies, or by the power of the spirit acting through the soul."

Paracelsus

"Imagination is more important than knowledge. For while knowledge defines all that we currently know and understand, imagination points to all we might yet discover and create."

Albert Einstein

The ability to imagine is universal and before anything manifests into form it is conceived in someone's mind through the power of imagination. Through our imagination, we co-create our lives, our health and wellness as well as dis-ease. All form is the outcropping of a mind and that is where the issue comes in because we do have preconceived notions. As Albert Einstein suggests, imagination points us to all the possibilities and when we are in the creative flow we are playing in the field of imagination.

As children our imagination was trivialized by well-meaning parents when they called it daydreaming or make-believe. In reality, it is a powerful tool and if more people understood this power they could transform their lives. It is our imagination that brings our hopes, dreams and desires into form. We are in a crisis of imagination because we have been so impacted by media and social programming to believe that it has no validity. It is time to reawaken our imagination and start creating the lives we want to live.

Deepak Chopra says, "Whatever you can see in your inner world, you can bring into existence in your outer world." The philosophy of the Law of Attraction takes this idea even further. It states that what we send out in thought and feeling is what manifests in our life. When you understand the Law of Attraction you see that vibration draws to itself like vibration. Without knowing it I created the illnesses and physical problems that I encountered but according to the

Law of Attraction I also created the new vision of my return to wellness. When we create unconsciously we are creating from programs that we are not even aware of. Such thoughts as "I am sick and tired of this job" can create "sick and tired" in our body. When I first tapped into the energy of the Inner Physician I was doing it from an unconscious level and each time I saw a problem change by connecting to that part of myself, it gave me more motivation to try it again. I have reached a point, through the process, where I make conscious choices to change my life.

Is magic just a metaphor? Is it really just sleight of hand and waving magic wands to produce rabbits, or are we all magicians capable of creating magical lives? Has the modern mind been commandeered by alien forces, as Marianne Williamson suggests? We have lost our magic powers and there is a way to remember what they are. We have a magical dream machine inside of us, we just need to remember how to access it. I believe each of us is a truly magical being with more power than we are aware of.

The word imagination is defined as the action of imagining or of forming mental images or concepts of what is not actually present to the senses. Those mental pictures plant seeds for what happens in the future, as your thoughts become reality. I have a vivid and active imagination, which has been a double-edged sword for me. As an artist and creative person it has been a great source of inspiration bringing me on journeys to my inner landscape, which have resulted in beautiful images. As an unconscious storyteller I have created a lot of unnecessary pain in my life as you have already seen as you read my story.

Imagination manifests reality and to the outside world it looks like magic. I have always loved magic. When I was a young girl I would watch magicians on television and marvel when they pulled a rabbit out of a hat or cut a woman in half and she came back whole. But there is more to magic than sleight of hand and making things appear and disappear. Magic can be defined as a mysterious quality of enchantment or invoking the supernatural. Some call it a miracle. If imagination manifests reality than everything in the world began in someone's mind. I hate to think that all the physical discomforts I have suffered were created in my mind. That seems like a huge responsibility and a masochistic thing to do.

Can you imagine that I created all of these bizarre stories that I just shared with you in my unconscious and they manifested in my reality? It only proves what a fabulous storyteller I am. My healing and transformation shows the power of the imagination to turn the story around and create a new reality. My inner movies provided me with information and symbols for the problems I encountered and lead me to uncovering the path to healing and so can yours. We have a choice. We can create positive stories or we can create negative stories and the one that you put your focus on is the one that will become real.

There is a way to create your life using story that is conscious and supportive. Once we dismantle the storytelling machine that is on negative autopilot and the unconscious fear that drives it we can use imagination and visualization in a positive way to manifest our dreams and desires. We can use this skill to create a reality that supports and nurtures us. Imagination, dreaming and visualization are good skills that have been used in the wrong way. If it is true that we are all great storytellers and that we create our reality through what we are thinking, why not think thoughts that create a reality that fulfills our desires. If it is true that the Universe always gives us what we are asking for, a vibrational match to what we are thinking and feeling, whether it is positive or negative, we might as well create from the positive and have a great time. That is a tall order when so much of our programming happened either preverbally or when we were children.

What if all of our Inner Physicians were helping us unravel those programmings so we could dream awake and aware and were using our various diseases to do that? If the world was filled with conscious dreamers it would be a different world. The day I was editing this chapter I broke my tooth. It was a "virgin tooth" meaning it didn't have a filling in it. It just popped while I was eating and I hadn't bitten into anything hard. I am extremely phobic of the dentist and consequently haven't seen one in many years.

Fortunately for me I am blessed with good strong teeth. I had to have the tooth pulled and be face to face with my biggest fear. When I started to look at it from a higher perspective I realized it was my Inner Physician getting me to go to the dentist and there wasn't any other way to make that happen but create a problem with my teeth that couldn't be ignored! I know this is true because even though my tooth was split right down the middle and part of it was really loose, I didn't feel any pain. I had moments of extreme fear and panic though, as I faced this lifelong fear and old programming head on and started to have routine dental care again.

I remember my own programming about dreaming my own reality when I was a child. I often heard my parents say to me, "Don't get your hopes up." I know they were coming from what they thought was a place of love, because they didn't want to see me disappointed and they were coming from their own experience where their dreams didn't come true. In reality they were killing my dreams without realizing it. I encourage you to not only get your hopes up, but to keep them up so you can create an environment where the Inner Physician can do its form of magic. Hope for the best possible outcome and think positive thoughts.

In the concept of the Inner Physician the communication between yourself and that part of you happens in the imagination usually through symbols. In my experience, it is clear that the relationship with the inner archetypal doctor is the crucial factor for the healing, because it is this inner involvement which is able to transform the symptom into a symbol or an image. The images are messages from the unconscious to consciousness, much as dreams are. Over a period of time, through asking the body what needs to be done, consulting the Inner Physician, you will begin to understand your own symbolic language and it will become clear what your personal symbols mean. You might find it helpful to consult a therapist or dream practitioner to help you understand the messages and symbols and keep a notebook with them and your discoveries about them in it.

Using the imagination to access the Inner Physician we are engaging an ally instead of giving all of the responsibility for our wellness to the doctor. It is important to form a partnership with your doctor and your Inner Physician. The practice of trusting only the doctor has in part been what has shut down the capacity to access the Inner Physician. When we are able to access our inner intelligence and find symbols, we can transform the symptom into an individual image or inner movie which will provide us with the understanding of what is needed in our healing process. For example you can imagine groups of Pac man figures going into your body and eating all of the cancer cells.

Such a method represents a modern form of the meditation the revolutionary Swiss physician Paracelsus (1493-1541) recommended five centuries ago, and the Medieval alchemists called the imaginatio vera. Paracelsus' words about the Inner Physician are shared in another chapter.

Magic, imagination, manifestation, quantum physics and synchronicity – these juicy words are interconnected for me. Within the words magic and imagination you find that they both contain the word magi. I remember the magi showing up at the birth of Jesus with gifts and I wonder what magicians were doing there. The word magi comes from the word magus, which was originally a priest but later misconstrued to be a sorcerer. The magus was a Zoroastrian astrologer-priest from ancient Persia who was able to tell the future, which is a form of magic. I can understand a priest being present at the birth of Jesus. Yet why not have magicians at the birth of Jesus, for he was a magician of the highest kind. His magic was manifest through miracles. I believe the Western translation for magician as sorcerer made many people think magic was something unreal, suspect and evil and that is why we have distanced ourselves from it and look at anyone who claims to do magic as suspect.

When we first start the process of conscious storytelling, visualizing a reality that we want to experience and it appears in our reality it looks like magic. In reality we are actually connecting with the divine and our visualization is like a prayer. I love the phrase "invoke the supernatural" because for me it suggests connecting with Source, the Creator, God and that way every thought becomes a prayer.

We can use visualization as a form of prayer and create a sacred container in which to create and manifest our dreams.

I think the word magic and synchronicity are synonymous. Synchronicity is defined by Jung as a meaningful coincidence of an external event with a psychic event, such as a dream, fantasy, or thought. These events coincide in time in a way that gives them meaning for the observer. That is, they seem like communications between a divine force and ourselves, and they confirm that there is a connection or interaction between our psyche and physical reality. When we are in the flow of the present moment synchronicity happens all of the time. Synchronicity and magic are the Universe's way of saying we are on the right path and they are happening every moment if we are conscious. Stay aware and pay attention to the magic because it is showing you the way to go that is right for you.

AWAKENING YOUR INNER PHYSICIAN

Try it for yourself. Take an issue you are struggling with and write it down in detail on a piece of paper and don't censor yourself. Look at it closely because this is the current story you are telling yourself and the Universe is supporting it. Are you surprised by your story? Is it more negative than you thought? This is because when you really allow yourself to write without censoring you get to the unconscious level and the unconscious story that is informing the Universe of your intentions. Ponder the message you are sending to the Universe through your story for a minute and think of examples of how the Universe has supported the story.

Now write a new story. Write down in detail what you would like to experience instead and don't censor yourself here either. Include sight, sounds, color and feelings so that it becomes more real. What are you wearing in the new story? What do you feel? How will it change your life? Why do you want this story to happen? Dig deep! This is your heart's desire. Begin telling the Universe that story and see what happens. Watch the synchronicity and magic begin to blossom around you. I bet you will be surprised.

I have included a guided meditation called "The Magical Dream Machine" on the Empowered Health and Wellness: Awakening Your Inner Physician CD. This meditation uses guided imagery to help you tap into your imagination so you can create a new story. You can order this CD at www.empoweredhealthandwellness.com.

CHAPTER TEN

Falling into Mastery

"Your body is made up of intelligent cells that are always bringing themselves into balance, and the better you feel, the less you are vibrationally interfering with the cellular rebalancing. If you are focused upon things that are bothering you, the cells of your body are hindered in their natural balancing process – and once an illness has been diagnosed and you then turn your attention to that illness, the hindering is greater still."

Abraham-Hicks

I thought that the book was finished when the events of this chapter took place. I thought I had learned everything there was to learn from my body and once again I was wrong. I had put together a query letter and my resume and was ready to search for a publisher for the book, but something felt incomplete. I found out after my accident what that was.

This chapter is different than all of the rest because I am writing in the midst of my recovery process not as a journalist writing about an event in retrospect. I feel that it is important to share all of my feelings and how I was able to shift them and return to wellness. I am typing with my non-dominant hand because the wrist on my dominant hand is broken and in a cast. I was a couple of days into the process as I began this chapter, a few days after I had surgery to repair the wrist. I trust that I will recover and that feeling will guide me to wellness. I have to type with one finger to put these words on the page, yet it feels important to do so. It is my intention to be transparent and real as I do this so you get the complete understanding.

It was August 8, 2008 (8-8-8), which was supposed to be an auspicious day. I drove 15 miles to the town where my friend Della lived so I could take her to lunch for her birthday. We had a lovely lunch and I had a margarita while we caught up because it had been a while since we had seen each other. After lunch we decided to go for a walk by the river and sit by the waterfall. I loved being by water, and sitting by a moving river near the waterfall was appealing.

I mentioned to her that I wished that I had brought my other shoes, which would be better for walking, but they were in my car a few miles away. We walked down a path toward the waterfall and onto a cement wall, which was about 5 feet high. I took several steps and with my next step there was nothing under me. I tumbled toward rocks and concrete below and there was nothing I could do but go with the fall. I didn't brace myself or try to grab something, because there was nothing to grab and I just plummeted. The fall was so quick that the next thing I knew I was on the rocks, lying on my side like a baby, as though something had caught me and placed me there. I didn't have time to be afraid or to utter a sound; there was no piercing scream or call for help, just silence as I fell. With the wall being 5 feet plus my height, my body fell just over 10 feet before I hit the rocks.

It was interesting to me that after I landed I lay very calm and centered. I fell, silently, ten feet to the rocks, landing like a baby, on a very auspicious day, 8-8-8. I was stunned. Remaining calm, I knew something important had just happened, though I had no idea what it was.

My friend and another woman ran to my side to see if I was okay. I wasn't sure, but I knew there was something wrong with my right arm and I gently placed it on my abdomen and would not let anyone touch it. We noticed a large egg forming on my left leg and cuts and scrapes were apparent. Della helped me to my feet and we began to walk to her car so she could take me to the hospital. I took several steps and the world started closing in around me as sound became muffled and the green grass below my feet turned gray and fuzzy. I told her I couldn't go any further or I would pass out and asked if she would call an ambulance as I sat down on the ground. My gray appearance made her respond quickly to my request. Within minutes I was surrounded by a fire truck, two police cars, a police truck and the paramedics and I felt embarrassed for the attention. They apparently thought I had fallen into the falls, a drop that would have been about 20 or 30 feet and would have killed me, had I teetered that direction instead of the direction I fell.

My arm remained glued to my tummy for safekeeping until I got into the ambulance, where I told the paramedics to be careful when they placed it in a sling. Once in the hospital I spent 3 hours on a hospital bed in the ER hallway because all the rooms were full and there were a couple of patients in critical condition so I wasn't a priority. The doctor determined I had fractured my wrist in two places. He took my arm in his hand and moved it and said, "It isn't as broken as I thought it would be." I was comforted by the range of motion I still had but when he said my bone was "smooshed" I was a bit concerned though I didn't get the impression that it was too bad. I guess "smooshed" is a relative term. When I was given a referral to an orthopedic surgeon I became suspicious. The doctor never attended to my legs or hips which were badly bruised and would later need attention too.

Monday morning I saw the orthopedic surgeon and I could see by the x-ray that it was a pretty bad fracture and decided that surgery was a better option to the unknowns that could happen if it was left to its own healing process. At 9 PM that night I was wheeled into surgery to have a titanium plate put into my arm to pull the fracture back into place. I left the hospital at 1:30 in the morning on Tuesday a few hours after my surgery was complete. When all was said and done I had my right arm in a cast, my arm pit and shoulder hurt, the bones in my knee were bruised and I had contusions which required a knee brace, and I couldn't get to sleep because of all the pain I felt.

When I got home my first thoughts were based on an experience of the past, an issue I had been holding on to since I was four years old. I had never had anyone joyfully take care of me and I always felt like a burden when I was hurt or sick. My thoughts began to create that reality. People were there to help but they were not happy to do it, there was tension and arguments and I wished I could just be alone to take care of myself like I usually did. The problem was, I couldn't, and I needed to find a way to surrender and receive care. I was frustrated that I would create this and cause problems for those around me. The more I thought about what wasn't going right the more I drew in what I didn't want. The more negative my thoughts were the more pain there was in my body. I was in a negative spiral moving in a direction that I didn't want to go.

I had been given some heavy-duty painkillers, the kind that people paid big money for on the street. I didn't like them but they did help me sleep and I vowed to get off of them as soon as possible because I could feel that they made it more difficult for me to remain positive and move in the direction of wellness. They actually made me feel agitated and more frustrated than normal. I would rather practice the Law of Attraction than take drugs for pain relief.

My understanding of the Law of Attraction is that disease and discomfort are the Law of Attraction's response to resistance. My immediate question was what am I resisting?

I felt so open and allowing at the time of the accident. It is interesting how quickly we move to the negative side of an issue. We are so programmed to think negatively or to err on the side of caution to protect ourselves from disappointment, that when we are stressed out we go into negative self-talk automatically. You rarely hear someone who has just fallen or had an accident, or upon finding they are diagnosed with a disease say, "This must be my lucky day" or "I am sure there is a fabulous reason for this happening," or "Isn't this wonderful, now I will get that much needed rest!" No, we go in the other direction of blame, shame, anger and frustration and none of those emotions have any healing power.

I wanted to analyze why I had fallen so I could understand why such a thing would happen now. That has always been the first step in my healing process. If I could figure it out I would have some sense of control. I had thoughts such as: "I should have listened to myself and changed shoes." "Did I call this to me through my vibration by talking about having the wrong shoes?" "I shouldn't have had the Margarita at lunch." "Why was I so dumb?" "How could I attract this when I thought I was in a great vibration?" "I guess I really don't know myself very well and I am not as evolved as I thought I was." Maybe I was being punished for putting off painting while I did other things and maybe I would never be able to paint again because of the broken arm. That thought made me really sad.

None of this thinking took me in the direction I wanted to go. I finally resolved myself to the fact that I fell and it didn't matter why. In fact my reasons were only stories that were making me feel bad and I would never know the reason why. I realized if I could create stories about why I fell, I could also create fabulous stories about how healthy and well I was too. It really didn't matter why I fell, what mattered now was that I moved toward feeling better and that could only happen one positive thought at a time.

I decided that I didn't want to talk about all the things that were going on that said I wasn't getting better. We tend to want to tell all of the gory details because we can get a lot of sympathy from people. Sympathy is only a temporary fix and it holds the negative story in place because now you have other people involved in the story.

Though I seemed to be drawing in exactly what I didn't want in terms of care I started saying to myself, "Everyone is doing the best they can, even me." I started to see all the good things that people were doing and became grateful for them. The energy around my care began to change and I began to be able to receive the assistance that I needed.

I kept thinking about something that happened a few weeks earlier when my daughter and I were on vacation in Chicago. I was in Chicago at an outdoor concert with Carrie and we were sitting on the grass. There were people all around us who had nice comfy folding chairs. I said, "Wouldn't it be nice if we had those nice folding chairs?" Carrie said, "Maybe next time." About 30 minutes later a man and his family came from out of nowhere. They had not been there when I made my comment. He came up to me with a folding chair and said, "I will not be able to enjoy the concert unless you are sitting in this chair." He opened the chair and I sat down and he walked over to his family and laid on a blanket and watched the concert. I was surprised and delighted at the instant manifestation! There were hundreds of people in the park that day and he came up to me soon after I made my statement! I wanted to tap into that feeling now when I needed to heal.

The feeling that comes from instant manifestation like that is incredible. It is the feeling of being open, trusting and in the flow. Magic happens in that space. I wanted to create my new affirmations on the energy of magic, surprise, delight and joy that would help me come back into homeostasis. I wanted my affirmations to ride into my nonconscious pathways on the feeling of wellness, and that was a tall order when I was feeling so much pain.

If I could manifest a chair that quickly I could bring my body back into well-being; all I had to do was change my thoughts. I had to be open to feeling better and trust that my body had the intelligence to make it so. The story of the chair became my mantra. It had been haunting me since it happened and now I knew why. It is as easy to instantly manifest a chair as it is to create health because all it takes is a focus on the desired outcome and alignment. Oh I make that sound so easy! So I started to repeat, "Wouldn't it be nice if my arm was in perfect health and I could drive and do everything I wanted to again?" Yes!

When you are in the middle of a very vivid life experience it is hard not to notice, especially if it has to do with discomfort and pain in your body. It takes a very powerful focus to ignore the what-is-ness of an illness. It is hard to move from physical pain into thinking positive thoughts about the future. Pain can keep you tethered to the present and make it difficult to tell yourself a new story. How could I say, "I am in perfect health and I feel wonderful," while my arm throbbed in my cast and my leg ached in my brace and my side hurt? If someone heard me they would have questioned my sanity. I could say, "Wouldn't it be nice if my arm were back to normal?" and "Wouldn't it be nice to feel healthy and strong again?" That is a great place to start in shifting vibration. It may sound like wishful thinking and that is okay because it brings in a new alignment with what you want and takes your focus away from what you don't want.

I knew I was being asked to step into mastery. I also knew that my body was in the hands of my wonderful Inner Physician who knew what it would take to knit my bone back together, heal the traumatized tissue in various areas of my body and bring me back into perfect health. I knew that stories of perfect health created a vibration and environment that would allow my body to heal. I put myself in its capable hands and moved as far as I could from my stories of woe, and into creating stories of perfect health and wellness. When I first wrote that sentence I misspelled the word woe using the word "whoa," which is interesting because it means "to halt" or "stop" and that is what I needed to do with my mind chatter. Knowing all of this didn't keep away the utter frustration, deep sadness and intense pain I felt at times. There were many times when I could not see how I could possibly heal from this trauma.

When I first began to recover small changes seemed monumental as I noticed I could move the tips of my fingers, which previously wouldn't move and I was grateful. I moved from clumsily chopping tomatoes with my non-dominant hand and a fork in my teeth to cutting beautiful slices using both hands, in just a few days! That was a miracle to be celebrated. I thought about the fall many times and was grateful that I hadn't had more injuries. I could have hit my head on the rocks, broken my neck, a leg or any number of things that would be worse than a fractured wrist.

The day I was able to blow dry my hair and put on makeup after two weeks of looking grungy was a great treat and another cause for celebration! I actually looked fabulous for the first time in several weeks and that sure helped in the recovery process. When I like the way I look I am more able to stay in a positive frame of mind. It might be a girl thing.

My new mantra/story became: "My body is a magical wellness machine. It has divine intelligence to know exactly how to come back into homeostasis. Every bone, muscle, joint and cell is in perfect harmony and alignment. All is well in my body." I also said things like, "Wouldn't it be nice to be able to drive again? Wouldn't it be nice to use my hand and feel great?"

As time went on and the range of motion was not returning to my wrist, it was hard to be positive. It was easy to think I was going to stay like this and that I was somehow being punished. I had put off painting for a time in the future and hadn't painted anything in two years. Was that now being taken away from me for procrastinating and not somehow making time? What was being called for was trust – the trust that another miracle could take place so that my hand and wrist could return to normal.

I was now relying on my own healing stories, from the chapters before this, as evidence that my body could heal. I had hoped the stories would help other people who were struggling with illness and now here they were helping me. I wrote them for someone else but the diary became a map for my own healing! I didn't need to solely rely on faking it till I made it. I could rely on my personal history of healing as evidence that healing even under the worst of circumstances was possible.

If I really wanted to embrace the Law of Attraction and create my own reality I had to let go of the story of what happened to cause my broken wrist. Without the story it was hard to know what to say to people when they asked what happened when they saw my arm in a cast. I have a juicy story that is somewhat exciting to tell, and elicits a lot of sympathy. We get nurtured by the sympathy we receive and it is hard to give that up. I wanted sympathy!! But retelling the story over and over reinforces the trauma, not the state of wholeness I want to achieve. Darn, good sympathy is hard to come by; oh well, it was not worth the cost.

Staying positive and focused on well-being was a real push toward mastery in the midst of pain in several areas of my body. One morning as I lay in bed I found a position that put me in a pain-free state and I stayed there for a long time focusing on how great that felt, how strong and flexible my body was, how I could move with grace and ease and how my body was in perfect alignment. I am told that it only takes 17 seconds of positive thinking to shift to a positive state and I was in this place for much longer than that. I was able to believe I was pain free and well and this was the path to regaining that state in my body.

Another morning I woke at 2:18 AM and couldn't get back to sleep. My right knee had gone into a muscle spasm that wouldn't let go and I could barely walk. I am sure it was from the trauma of the fall. It hurt so bad I forgot about my broken wrist, unless I needed to use it. Now I had pain in my armpit, wrist and leg, all on the right side which is the side of the impact of the fall. I was in pain and I couldn't get myself to believe anything else. I tried thinking about the parts of my body that didn't hurt but that didn't hold my attention long. A hot bath didn't shift things like it usually does. I was looking for a positive string that I could pull on to get me back on track. YouTube videos pulled me out of my downward spiral. If you haven't gone on to YouTube it is a must. You can access it at any time of the day or night and find a video on any subject.

For my purpose I wanted to shift into positive thinking so I looked for anything about the Law of Attraction and health and wellness. I found a number of videos on the subject and watched them. This was the inspiration I needed and I began to see the Law of Attraction in action as my thoughts shifted to thoughts about feeling good. I realized that I was not alone, and that there are many beings on the other side supporting my return to wellness. I was inspired to get an ice pack and put it on my knee. I couldn't even think about the ice pack when I was in pain so this felt like a revelation. I climbed back into bed with the ice pack, propped my knee up on a stack of pillows, put on an Abraham CD and drifted off to sleep at 4:30. When I woke up I felt better. The pain was reduced and if I walked really slow it didn't feel bad. I broke through and was on the other side and after another ice pack I felt pretty good. Now I could start to generate positive thoughts about getting well again. If I can manifest a chair instantly I can certainly heal my body!

Three weeks after I fell I woke up thinking it was time to forgive my mother who wasn't there for me when I was in the hospital as a four-year-old and needed her the most. I had made a commitment at 4 years of age to take care of myself and not trust anyone else to help me. This had gotten in the way of my receiving care and nurturing long enough. Holding her hostage to the incident was holding me hostage as well. She didn't even know I had feelings that I had been carrying around all these years so it was really only impacting me. The pain I felt in my knee and leg was a real metaphor for not being able to move forward. I wouldn't truly be able to move forward until I resolved this issue.

As I thought about it, I realized my mother came from a long line of women who didn't know how to nurture or be emotionally present so it was an issue that was in my tissues, bloodline and bones. The bones hold the deepest of memory so it seemed appropriate that I broke one of my bones and this ancestral issue was pouring out. I knew that if I could shift this I would be able to allow well-being and my dreams and desires to come into my life and, in the process, transform this issue for generations to come.

I began to do Ho'oponopono, the ancient practice of forgiveness from Hawaii. This is a practice of forgiveness that is focused on you, not outside circumstances. I could feel things shifting as I felt sadness, nausea and then a sense of peace. I actually started seeing my mother through a different set of eyes, understanding that she did the best she could with the skills she had. For the first time in the years that I had worked on this issue I felt a sense of hope. In reality this was a reflection of where I was not taking care of myself, because of the issue of lack of nurturing and lack of care in my bloodline. As I thought about this from a nonjudgmental prospective I realized that I had received messages from my internal guidance system that I shouldn't go for a walk in the shoes I was wearing. I heard the message and repeated it out loud and yet I kept walking and in fact argued with myself about it, just like I had when I had a car accident years ago. We receive messages all of the time from our guidance system to help us navigate and keep us out of harm's way. When I don't listen to my internal messages I am not taking care of myself. When I don't listen to that part of me that knows from a higher prospective I am perpetuating the very thing that I don't want and that always calls in more of the same which, in this case, was lack of care and self-nurturance.

The following day I woke up inspired. I decided to try an herbal body wrap, which I sell, on my leg to see if it would help the pain. I wrapped my knee and left it on for several hours. Within the first hour the pain was reduced to about 20% of what I had been feeling! I imagine that it was removing toxins and inflammation from my knee and that accounted for the pain relief. It was exciting to discover the pain- relieving qualities of a product that I was already sold on.

When I went to the physical therapist and she discovered I was an artist she told me to start painting. I hadn't thought about painting as a way to rehabilitate my hand because I didn't know that it would be helpful. Now the idea was dancing in me. I decided to do a small watercolor every few days to see what happened. I knew I could paint joy, well-being and wellness and I didn't have to pretend. I am a visionary artist so I can bring myself to the place where I am immersed in those feelings and bring them to life on paper.

If they are alive on paper they are alive in me. I was surprised with the ease at which I could paint even though I was still wearing a splint. The painting called "Joy" flowed from my splinted hand in a new way, more free-flowing and less controlled than past paintings. I loved the feel of the brush in my hands and pushing the color around to mix and create new colors on the paper. The painting filled my being with joy and I know wellness and well-being on all levels was not far behind.

Exactly four weeks from the day I had fallen I had one of several big breakthroughs. In this case "break" takes on several meanings. By this time I had a brace on my right knee and a brace on my right arm, which put me in a vulnerable place physically and emotionally. I was in touch with how I can't drive and have to have people help me and I was in touch with how helplessness and vulnerability really feel. I could really relate to how I felt as a four-year-old when I was sick and in the hospital and my mother didn't come to visit me. Because my mother had let me down I believed that everyone would. I made a commitment to be self-sufficient and that is what I have done all of my life. I needed to feel this in order to let go of the complex I created because it was holding me back from experiencing a life of joy.

All week I had been in a weepy mood and really in touch with needing to forgive myself. One morning I said to a friend, "I realize I have been very hard on people, because I am also so hard on myself." She was ecstatic that I would finally come to this realization and congratulated me for being open enough to say it. I cried. I cried for me and I cried for all the people who have passed through my life that I have been so hard on: my kids, mother, family, and friends. I could feel the energy around me shifting as I acknowledged this and understood the great impact this would have on my life. It took this fall to break this loose from inside of me. I also knew that healing would now be fast and easy because I had learned what I needed to learn.

Another setback happened when I wasn't getting my range of motion back even though I was in physical therapy twice a week. I had 90 degrees of movement in my left wrist and 45 degrees in my right wrist. I was angry and disappointed. My physical therapist told me that I might stay that way and I might not get any more movement. I looked at her and said, "Never say never to Katelyn Mariah!" Now I had the internal conviction to prove her wrong. She had to be wrong because my wrist was locked at 45 degrees and wasn't going any farther and that was unacceptable.

Two months into my return to wellness I had one of those early morning breakthroughs that come like a bolt of lightning. I realized I had fallen because I lost my balance and this was a metaphor for how I was out of balance in my life. Not only was my life out of balance but I felt like I had fallen off my true path. I was in survival mode focused on meeting basic needs, working 22 hours a week as a psychologist and building a residual income business so all I did was work. I had become industrialized. My dreams were on hold until that magic day when I had enough money to stop holding my breath. Yes I wanted financial freedom,

I wanted love in my life, time to create, time to travel and time to dream and all I did was work. What was called for now was not only a miracle of healing but me finding a way to bring balance back into my life.

Once I realized that my life was out of balance and began to do things to change that, a shift happened as is usually the case. I had gone to the orthopedic surgeon for a follow up and he was concerned about my range of motion too and offered that a cortisone shot might help. I wasn't too keen on cortisone because I heard it wasn't good for your joints but I was desperate for this to change.

The doctor left the room for a moment and came back with the shot in hand, much to my surprise, and before I could say anything it was being pushed into my wrist. The pain was so strong that I began to cry. This was the first time I had cried during this entire event. Now the flood gate was opened and I felt like I was releasing 2 1/2 months of sadness. The pain from the shot lasted for more than 8 hours. A few days later I noticed that my wrist was moving more freely. When I went to the physical therapist I was almost afraid to say I felt I was making progress and indeed

I was. I had gained 16 degrees in my range of motion and I knew from that point that my hand would return to normal.

I worked on bringing balance back to my life and have regained all of my range of motion. When I am in balance I have more range of motion in every area of my life. At exactly 4 months from the date of my surgery, my doctor released me from his care because he felt I was doing amazing. He was surprised that I had so much movement and that I could squeeze my left hand with 56 pounds of pressure and my right hand was only a pound behind! This seems like another miracle to me.

Once again I can say that I feel like this accident turned out to be a gift because I was able to realize and release some very old patterns that were holding me back. As an active participant in this healing experience, rather than a journalist writing after the fact, I realized that it is not easy to heal. It takes courage and conviction not to fall into the throes of an illness or injury and succumb. I have gotten really good at working with the Law of Attraction and healing my body and even with all my experience I still found it difficult to stay positive at the time. I am thankful for my support system, both internal, external and in unseen realms for helping me get back on track when I lost my way.

It is not easy to maintain a positive focus when you are in physical pain. It is important to surround yourself with people who love and support you. Tell them that what you really need help with is staying focused on health and well-being. Ask them to be reflections of well-being for you, and when you get off track ask them to help you get centered again. Find doctors who can do the same thing. Find someone you trust who will support you to use all forms of healing modalities, a healing coach of sorts. Trust that these people will help you stay on track on your path to wellness and don't be afraid to ask for help.

We will explore other ways to detoxify mind, body and spirit next.

To learn more about the Ultimate Body Applicator, the herbal body wrap which I used for pain relief, see the resource section in the back of the book under Your Body Ecologist.

CREATIVE TECHNIQUE FOR WELLNESS

Detoxification: Mind, Body, and Spirit

"Spiritual progress is like detoxification. Things have to come up in order to be released. Once we have asked to be healed then our unhealed places are forced to the surface."

Marianne Williamson

"Although the body is normally quite capable of detoxing on its own, rising stress levels, lack of exercise, constipation, and poor diet and lifestyle choices – not to mention the ever-increasing levels of toxins in the environment – can push it to capacity."

Cathy Wong, ND

Harmony in our external relationships begins by establishing harmony within our body mind and spirit. I am a huge proponent of detoxification as a way of bringing harmony and balance back into the body. Many people don't understand the importance of detoxification and as the quotes above express we can be toxic physically, mentally, emotionally and spiritually. We usually think of detoxification as the process of removing toxins from inside the body to achieve a greater level of health and wellbeing, which is true. What most people don't realize is that our minds can also become incredibly toxic. I saw how people were impacted by toxins when I worked as a psychologist. When their thinking was out of harmony they were often also physically sick too. Depression, anxiety and other disorders are often a result of how we are thinking. The outside world is a reflection of the interior world.

Toxins in the Mind

Toxins in our mind are simply negative thoughts that keep us from moving forward with our dreams and goals. We all have negative thoughts so that isn't the issue. Negative thoughts become a problem when we spend more of our time feeling hopeless, depressed, frustrated, and stuck than we do feeling hopeful, loving, joyful and abundant. In the consciousness of creating our own reality it is believed that thoughts become things, and if we focus on what we don't want we continue to create more of that in our lives. We are always creating our reality and it is always manifesting, even when it manifests as things we didn't want to experience. I hope you can be open minded when you think about your disease and the possibility you created it as an experience to learn something on a higher level. I know it is not what you want to hear but it might reveal a transformational lesson if you remain open to the possibility.

How does this work in the context of our health? How do toxic thoughts have an impact on our body? Here are a few examples to illustrate this point.

"He gives me a pain in my neck!"

"I am sick and tired of this!"

"This makes me so angry I can't even see straight!"

Something "eating at you" could manifest as cancer.

You get the idea. The Inner Physician is listening and acting accordingly. If you continue to affirm these statements eventually you will start to have pain in your neck, feel fatigue and have problems with your vision. Thinking and health goes deeper than those simple metaphors because we have many thoughts that we are not even conscious of. Here are a few examples of how we can pick up thoughts that can become toxic and impact our health and wellness.

Have you noticed in the past several years that many of the commercials on mainstream television are about medications? Many start out by describing a symptom and how this drug will relieve it and end by rapidly talking about all of the horrible side effects, so fast that you stop paying attention. At the very end, each of them says something like, "If you experience any of these symptoms see your physician."

These commercials are actually programming people to become sick. What happens is you feel one of the symptoms, remember the commercial and start thinking you might have such and such disease. If you aren't aware of it you can actually program your body to manifest that disease. My mother told me once that she saw a drug on television directed toward something she was feeling and she asked her doctor if he would prescribe it. Bingo! That is how the program works!

Forgiveness is a great way to detoxify the mind. There is a Hawaiian healing technique called Ho'oponopono which is an ancient code of forgiveness, used to correct the things that went wrong in a person's life. The translation of Ho'oponopono is "Making things Right." Right Thinking + Right Action = Right Future, which sounds like the Law of Attraction to me. It is sometimes referred to as simply ho'opono, and is a concept, a value and a related set of practices that have been used in Hawaiian and other Polynesian cultures for centuries to support harmonious relationships between people, nature and Spirit.

Ho'oponopono has been popularized by Joe Vitale and Dr. Ihaleakala Hew Len, PhD in Joe's book, Zero Limits, which I recommend that you read. It may sound preposterous, but taking personal responsibility for everything in your life can change everything. Dr. Len says, "There is no such thing as out there. Everything exists as thoughts in my mind." Many great teachers through history have had this same philosophy. Ho'oponopono is so powerful because it targets the root cause of unhappiness and pain which is the source of dis-ease. Essentially, it means to make it right with the ancestors, or to make right with the people with whom you have relationships. The main purpose of the process is to discover the Divinity within oneself and the Inner Physician is a part of that Divinity.

The late Hawaiian Kahuna, Morrnah Nalamaku Simeona created an updated version of Ho'oponopono, which is called Self-I-Dentity Ho'oponopono. This technique points out the importance of taking personal responsibility for everything you encounter in life, good or bad. Self-I-Dentity Ho'oponopono teaches strategies for cleaning the negative energies within yourself and not projecting them on to people outside of you. If it is showing up in your field you are somehow a part of it. It helps clear out old memories and accompanying thoughts to make way for more self-empowering thoughts, which support the manifestation of positive experiences.

The most important beginning step to any healing technique is cleansing, whether we are working on the mental, physical, emotional or spiritual level. This kind of clearing can be likened to a physical detoxification where we do a cleansing to remove chemicals and toxins from the liver or other organs, only this cleansing is in the mind.

I have used Ho'oponopono many times and have seen almost immediate results. Part of why I think it works so well is because you don't have to figure anything out, dissect or analyze an issue to understand it like we are used to doing. Let's say a conflict comes up between you and another person. Instead of analyzing it to figure out whose issue it is, you own the fact that part of the issue is yours and you do the process. It basically bypasses the mind and goes straight to the heart, which wants to resolve issues so it can return to harmony. When we engage the mind in analyzing we keep energy going that doesn't serve the purpose we are looking for. I remember in the past how we used to "process" everything and it took weeks, months and sometimes years to transform an issue. This "processing" kept us stuck. Ho'oponopono is instantaneous not only impacting you but the person or issue you are clearing.

Negative thoughts are toxic and they create a toxic environment where disease can thrive. Ho'oponopono is about restoring your light! It is a simple process of letting go of any toxic energies and allowing a new space for the healing power of your true Divine Thoughts, the Inner

Physician, to take action. When we clear out toxic thoughts we raise our vibration. Dis-ease cannot live in a high vibrational environment.

One of the most important components to Ho'oponopono is the Hawaiian belief that forgiveness must be given, if asked for. Ask and you shall receive is another principle found in the Bible and in the Law of Attraction. Forgiveness in Hawaiian is Kala, which means clearing the path or cutting the cord between the two people or events involved.

Along with the updated Ho'oponopono process, Morrnah was guided to include the three parts of the self, which are the key to Self I-Dentity. These three parts, which exist in every molecule of reality, are called the Unihipili (child/subconscious), the Uhane (mother/conscious), and the Aumakua (father/super conscious). It is as though we carry the sum total of our family and what we learned from them inside us. This is similar to Carl Jung's archetypes for the unconscious mind. When this "inner family" is in alignment, a person is in rhythm with the Divine and in the flow of life and magnetic to positive life experiences. Ho'oponopono helps restore balance in the individual first, and then in all of creation.

Why do we need to forgive our ancestors? Most of the programs we are operating with have been passed down from generation to generation and given to us as children. As children we believed in the kindness of people around us and we believed that our parents had our best interest at heart. They taught us from the perspective that they knew to be true. We believed what we learned from adults was the truth because we didn't know anything else and we depended on them for guidance. In the process we repressed our desires and our innate ability to tap into our inner wisdom. It is not that the programs were bad, they worked at some point in history, but they are not working now. Through forgiveness we release our parents and those old programs' impact on us. This is akin to clearing out karma. Couple forgiveness with gratitude and you have a powerful technique. With gratitude we acknowledge all the wonderful things in our lives and show our true appreciation for them. The true test of Ho'oponopono's power is if you can see the person or think about them without feeling any negative emotions. If you feel negative emotions it means there is still work to do.

If we are responsible for all things in our existence then we also have the power to diminish or allow things to grow simply by showing gratitude or forgiveness.

Forgiveness clears out obstacles and Gratitude feeds our desires. When doing Ho'oponopono you are not asking for forgiveness from someone outside you, it is you that the technique is directed at. It is not about forgiving someone for wrongdoing, it is about clearing negative memories, blocks and energies out of you.

Let's look at the steps of the Ho'oponopono technique beginning with this beautiful prayer created by Morrnah:

"Divine creator, father, mother, son as one ... If I, my family, relatives and ancestors have offended you, your family, relatives and ancestors in thoughts, words, deeds and actions from the beginning of our creation to the present, we ask your forgiveness ... Let this cleanse, purify, release, cut all the negative memories, blocks, energies and vibrations and transmute these unwanted energies to pure light ... And it is done."

Different practitioners have different methods of invoking the power of Ho'oponopono, some more elaborate than others. Dr. Joe Vitale utilizes a method of invoking Ho'oponopono which can be summed up in the 4 phrases that he uses whenever he wants to invoke Ho'oponopono, which is also called "cleaning." This is the version that I use. You don't say the words in parenthesis.

"I'm Sorry." *(I am sorry I forgot who I truly am, my Divine self. I am sorry for any unconscious intention I have that has created my current situation.)*

"Please Forgive Me" *(for not knowing or for my unconscious thinking).*

"I Love You" *(you are saying this to yourself and it activates the healing).*

"Thank You" *(this is the gratitude piece).*

260

While saying the phrases above, visualize the colors indigo, ice blue and white. Ho'o'pono'pono uses these colors to represent a transformation from dark to light. You must visualize an item, person or even a space/place being bathed in each of the colors starting with indigo and moving to white. Once the process is complete and the subject is filled and surrounded with white light the vibration is also higher.

This is a simple yet powerful practice. The Hawaiians use this technique as a ritual at the end of the day before they retire, to clear out problems of the day. If you do this every night and whenever you are in the midst of an issue you will always have a clear path.

Using Ho'oponopono I was able apologize to my higher self for the unconscious beliefs and intentions that caused me to get sick. I forgave myself for not being aware of them and loved myself despite what I created in my body. This self-love turns the key for healing to begin. This removes blame because we are acknowledging the problems were created in our unconscious and not on purpose.

Can it really be that simple? Yes, it can. If you think about it if we are constantly thinking negative thoughts about a particular issue it is impossible for anything positive to happen. It also makes sense that if we have positive thoughts about something that kind of environment is fertile soil for good things to grow. Ho'oponopono acts like a homeopathic remedy going to the source and clearing out the problem.

Detoxifying The Body

Toxins in our body create an environment for disease and if we become ill while it's

in a toxic state it makes it harder to get well. The body has to be detoxified in order for it to function properly and to promote health and well-being, yet surprisingly there is very little talk about it. I have never had a doctor ask me if I was doing a routine detoxification, have you?

Detoxing is particularly important in the modern world, since environmental pollutants, toxins and other elements can quickly build up to toxic levels and cause ill health as well as a variety of mental and physical consequences. These serious consequences include such things as weakened immune systems, inflammation, fatigue and depression.

We unknowingly consume toxic compounds directly into our systems, especially if we eat processed foods. If we are not purchasing organic foods our fruits and vegetables can have inorganic pesticides built into them and they can cause problems in our body. Add GMOs to the mix and it is no wonder so many people are sick! Toxins also come from air pollution in the environment and chemicals in our clothing and cleaning products. These toxins can invade the lymph, digestive and intestinal systems, our skin and our hair and compromise our health. Studies show that most Americans have somewhere between 400 and 800 chemicals stored in their bodies, typically in fat cells. Wow! Our fat cells are actually a protective device created to keep the toxins from going into our vital organs. We don't realize that we are being affected by them until we get a chronic disease after years of subtle and often consistent exposure to a combination of these toxins. I use a large herbal patch in my detoxification that you can read about in the resource section.

Detoxification has been understood and practiced for centuries by many cultures across the globe, including Chinese medicine, in which detoxification includes resting, nourishing and cleansing the body from the inside out. As a culture we are just beginning to understand its importance, beyond the rigid fasts that people have done to cleanse their bodies. While it is impossible to completely avoid toxins, it is important to find ways to support the body to get rid of them on a regular basis. Detoxing is something that can be done every day and doesn't have to be relegated to once or twice a year of heavy toxin release that can be painful and leave you feeling sick for several days.

Homeostasis is the ability of the body to maintain balance and there is a natural process of detoxification that occurs all the time, but because of the increase in toxins in the environment our body can't keep up with the process. There is a natural flux and flow of chemical reactions within every cell of every living organism that helps keep our systems in balance. The human body has trillions cells with approximately 35,000 chemical reactions taking place per second, and many of them involve healing and repair. Imagine throwing toxins into that mix and a new set of chemicals for the body to contend with. I think you get the picture; toxins disturb the natural flux and flow of homeostasis. The body's immune system must defend against these toxins and the battle between homeostasis and the immune system often expresses as disease.

I use Greens, an alkalizing powder that I add to coconut water every morning before I eat. This does a gentle internal detoxification every day so toxins don't build up in my body the way they would if I didn't take it. There are other natural detoxes you can do daily, such as fresh lemon in warm water, which helps detoxify and boost the immune system. I combine this with the It Works Ultimate Body Applicator for a complete detox inside and out.

There are so many ways to cleanse and detoxify your body and whole books have been written about them. I encourage you to find one that works for you and add it to your lifestyle, especially if you are in the midst of a healing process. Give your body what it needs and it will return you to balance and wellness.

AWAKENING YOUR INNER PHYSICIAN

Here is how you can put your Inner Physician into action to help you eliminate toxic thinking.

Awareness is the first step in moving toward a state of health so if you are aware of what you are thinking you are on the right track. To get a clearer understanding of where you are in your thinking it is good to take a piece of paper and start writing everything that is coming up in relation to your thoughts and your health. It is not necessary to discover everything. Anything you come up with is a great place to start and will more than likely take you to other things.

You might discover things that are recent and some that go back into your past. All of these unresolved, incomplete personal mental and emotional issues are poisoning your cells, acidifying your body and causing you to age and get sick. You want to release them.

The best way to release them is through forgiveness. My favorite method is Ho'oponopono, because of its simplicity. I have found in my experience that processing and rehashing the past is not helpful and this technique allows you to forgive without doing those things.

The most important part of the process is letting go so you can heal. Letting go is an ongoing process and part of being human. There will always be things that happen in our lives that cause discomfort, but hanging on to them is what causes toxins followed by disease. The best way to be healthy and happy is to live in the moment and always be mindful of thoughts that are causing toxicity.

Take an inventory of the kinds of foods you are eating. Which ones are contributing to health and wellbeing and which are not? You can dive right into a new eating program and eliminate all the toxic foods or you can do it gradually. Anything you do in the right direction will have an impact. Do the same thing with your environment and start making changes there too. You will soon see the difference this makes in your health.

CREATIVE TECHNIQUE
FOR WELLNESS

Attracting Health and Wellness

"We can appeal to Divinity, who knows our personal blueprint, for healing of all thoughts and memories that are holding us back at this time. It is a matter of going beyond traditional means of accessing knowledge about ourselves."

Morrnah Simeona

"A problem is only a problem if we say it is. And a problem is not the problem ~ how we react to the problem is the problem."

Dr. Ihaleakala Hew Len

"Wellness that is being allowed, or the wellness that is being denied, is all about the mindset, the mood, the attitude, the

practiced thoughts. There is not one exception, in any human or beast; because, you can patch them up again and again, and they will just find another way of reverting back to the natural rhythm of their mind. Treating the body really is about treating the mind. It is all psychosomatic. Every bit of it, no exceptions."

Abraham-Hicks, from the workshop 5/13/08

There are three Universal Laws that are important here, the Law of Attraction, the Law of Allowing and the law of Deliberate Creation and Ho'oponopono addresses all of them.

The Law of Allowing is about allowing everyone around you to live the life they choose even though it is different than how you live. Abraham says that the Art of Allowing is "finding a vibration that feels SO good when you find it, feels better and better as you maintain it, and gives you evidence of that connection through THRIVING. The immediate response of that connection is joy in the moment (NOW). The long range evidence is abundance in all things you consider good – like health, relationships, and dollars. The truth is, there is freedom in allowing circumstances to be what they are and people to be who they are, whether you agree with them or not. Even when it comes to poverty or war or disease."

The Law of Allowing also means allowing for perfect health and opening up and allowing it in because you deserve to be healthy. How many of us think about allowing health in, especially when we are sick? In recent years when I start to feel I am coming down with something I do whatever I can not to think about it and instead think about perfect health. When I can hold positive thoughts I often am sick for a day and then it is gone. The act of allowing creates flow and a magnetic field of attraction which actually draws health to you. Finally the Law of Deliberate Creation means consciously choosing what you want to experience and thinking the thoughts to make it happen. The Law of Deliberate Creation is simply understanding the Law of Attraction and then consciously and deliberately choosing the thoughts and emotions that feel better. It is always about reaching for the thought that feels better from right where you are.

The Law of Attraction and creating your own reality are all the rage these days as though they are new concepts. Theories of creating your reality are ancient but are only recently being rediscovered. In 1957 a physicist at Princeton, Hugh Everett, III, discovered through his research that for every moment of our lives there are many moments, possibilities and outcomes playing out simultaneously and present for every choice in our lives. Though we may not be aware of them they are all happening at the same time as the reality we are experiencing. Everett called these realities parallel possibilities. Science fiction jumped on the idea and began writing it into books and movies creating the illusion that it was only fantasy.

There is an age-old theory that all possibilities are already created and we just choose them by what we align with. Thoughts become things when you add feeling and emotion to them. According to the Law of Attraction there is no separation between the past, present and future. We align with new realities by becoming magnetic and we become magnetic by visualizing the reality and becoming it by feeling it as if it already exists. These concepts are being revived by quantum theorists such as Gregg Braden and Deepak Chopra. Chopra states that desire is pure potentiality seeking manifestation. I have always viewed desire as the fuel that carries us along our path and without it we wouldn't be motivated to live. Desire can be a trap or an ecstatic journey.

In Gregg Braden's book, The Isaiah Effect, he suggests that when we focus on one of those possibilities out of the many, what we focus on becomes our reality. This is true on a personal level as well as a large global scale. What this implies is that for every moment of catastrophe the prophets see in our future, while they may well be possible consequences of the choices we are making in our lives right now, there are other outcomes just as possible. We imagine a possibility long enough and it will manifest in our reality according to quantum physics. For every illness we create there are many outcomes and solutions to its resolution. Do we choose health and wellness or do we focus on how bad we feel? Many of us who are working with these principles are finding that magic is happening in our lives. I have discovered over and over that if I choose to heal and think positive thoughts I can change conditions in my body that I was told would never change. My healing stories are proof to quantum theory.

According to Braden, "This is where the boundaries between spiritual traditions, religions, quantum physics and philosophy become very fuzzy. One of the things we've been told by proponents of 'new thought' is that we create our reality. What quantum science now says, and what I believe the ancients were saying, is that that is close, but not completely accurate. Rather, for every moment in our lives we live a great many simultaneous possibilities that are all playing out in time. They are essentially dormant in our cosmos, sleeping until we awaken them through choices we make. All our individual choices then become our collective response to a given time in history."

According to the Law of Attraction, everything that we feel, see, think, touch, smell or hear are things that we created ourselves. They are a reflection of our inner world of thoughts. The Law of Attraction is the attractive, magnetic power of the Universe that draws similar energies together. It manifests through the power of creation, everywhere, in everything and in multiple ways. The Law of Attraction manifests through your thoughts, by drawing to you thoughts and ideas of a similar kind or vibration, people who think like you, and corresponding situations and circumstances. As the Bible says, "you reap what you sow." Have you ever noticed that when you change, the people in your life often do too? They either leave your life or they make changes in themselves. That is the Law of Attraction at work.

It is hard to swallow this concept when it comes to illness. It is hard to accept that we have created disease. I don't like the idea that I was fully responsible for creating all the pain and discomfort I created. You might even want to throw this book across the room right now rather than ponder that idea. It might be hard for you to buy into the concept of the Law of Attraction, but I encourage you to be open to the idea of creating a new mental environment that is conducive of healing. Try it for just 30 minutes if it is really hard for you to buy, and see what happens.

The Law of Attraction, which is an ancient belief, is growing in popularity today, thanks to movies like "The Secret," which is a bit too simplistic as far as I am concerned. There is a lot more to do than think something into reality. We can't say "Om" and watch a banana appear in our hand. Yet. But the movie and book opened people to a new level of awareness as to the possibility that we create our own reality.

The idea behind the Law of Attraction is not new. The concept can be found in Hinduism and it influenced Theosophy so you can find it mentioned in early Theosophical texts. An influential modern book on the subject in the English language is As a Man Thinketh by James Allen (1864 - 1912), which was published in 1902. The title for the book comes from the ancient Jewish Book of Proverbs, chapter 23, verse 7: "As a man thinketh in his heart, so he is." What we think, and send out on our emotions, from the heart, is what we attract into our lives.

Simply stated, our thoughts create our reality and like attracts like. We think both positive thoughts and negative ones to create contrast so that we can discover what it is that we truly want in our lives. Before I knew about the Law of Attraction I had an idea that I might be able to reach my ideal body weight by affirming the weight that I wanted to be. Instead of saying "I am fat," or "I have big hips and a fat stomach" every time I looked in the mirror I would say, "I weigh 135 pounds." I didn't do anything with my diet or exercise; I just said the affirmation. Over a period of months I reached my goal of weighing 135 pounds. I noticed that the more I said the affirmation the more I automatically changed my eating habits and desire to exercise, without realizing it. My mind began to think thoughts that would support me to lose weight and my thoughts changed so that I was doing things to make it happen.

Esther and Jerry Hicks have written about the Law of Attraction long before it became popular. Esther brings forth the teaching of a group of nonphysical beings that she calls Abraham. Abraham's sole purpose is to teach us that we can create the kind of life we desire by changing our thoughts and the things we focus on. What we focus on we become. Abraham lovingly tells us that we make things more difficult than they need to be and creating the reality we want to experience is as easy as changing your thoughts and the emotions attached to them.

The good news in all of this is that if we are responsible for all things in our existence, that includes the good things as well as the bad things. It also means we can change the things in our life that we don't like. Let's look at the idea of creating illness for a minute. No one wants to believe that they would create something that would cause them pain. The genius in creating illness is that it creates huge contrast and shows you without a doubt what you don't want. Illness happens slowly over time, through an unconscious stream of thoughts that create an environment for it. The thoughts might be so subtle that you can't see them without something big coming into your field to shine a light on them, such as illness. Once you can see the contrast and the thoughts that created it, you can begin to focus on healing.

AWAKENING YOUR INNER PHYSICIAN

Who do you need to do Ho'oponopono about that may be connected to your current illness? The connection to your illness might not be clear cut so take time to make a list of people and events that cause you irritation. Also think about judgments that you hold because they are a good indicator of a need for forgiveness on your part. Spend time over the next week doing Ho'oponopono with the issues you have identified and then make note of how those people or events have changed in your eyes or notice the evidence of change that you are now experiencing.

CHAPTER ELEVEN

Awakening the Sleeping Giant

"I fear we have awakened a sleeping giant and filled him with a terrible resolve."

Isoroku Yamamoto

I am resolved to finish this book before I have any more physical issues to write about! I know, I have said this before but this time it is true. This book needs to get out into the world and touch people. I don't need any more stories to share to show that healing is possible. I think I have shown you that already.

Anyway, a year ago when I was working on the book to get it finished I had another car accident that left me with whiplash and a concussion. Of course it gave me many opportunities to learn about myself, but also to discover a new healing modality that others might find helpful.

Of course two cars hitting at 50 miles an hour would turn my brain upside down! I realized about a week into this concussion that the accident had really woken up a sleeping giant, which was a concussion that happened 4 years earlier that I wrote about in an earlier chapter. If you recall I had fallen from a 5-foot wall onto a hillside of boulders running along the river. At the time, I broke my wrist and needed a titanium plate put in to repair it. No one thought about my head and possible injury, including me. Thinking back, my memory wasn't the same after the fall, but I didn't notice it because I was on heavy pain medication for a couple of weeks and there was no transition. I didn't notice that my mind had changed.

I have always prided myself on having great recall, having the ability to see an issue from many angles, and being able to analyze and figure things out with ease. Not being able to do that was frustrating … at first. For days after the accident I struggled to find the right words and had gaps where there were no words at all when I wanted to complete a sentence. I also prided myself on being smart, so looking not so smart was a challenge.

I realized quickly that this accident was unleashing a sleeping giant that probably included two previous concussions that were never diagnosed. Both occurred at the same time as I had broken bones and the bones were the main focus of my treatment. No one even thought of checking my head four years ago when I fell about 9 feet from a retaining wall onto boulders on the side of the river. I slammed into the ground and I am not sure where my head went in the process. I ended up with a broken wrist that had to be surgically repaired with Titanium which is what saved me from serious head injuries.

Last year I fell down the stairs in the dark and broke my toe on the edge of the door as I slammed my head into the wall. It was the same feeling in my head that I had when I stood up and almost dropped to the floor that I had when I stood up after slamming into the ground.

When I started working with the chiropractor who works specifically on concussions I had the same feeling when I stood to get off the table after our first treatment. She works with Frequency Specific Microcurrent and has had a lot of success reversing concussions. My doctor told me that the currents restore the innate balance of the cells in the body by using currents that are specific to that part of the body.

FSM, or Frequency Specific Microcurrent, is a new treatment that supplies our cells with extra free electrons and protons. Using frequency specific resonance to remove pathologies and repair tissue, and micro-amperage current to increase energy production in the cells, the body's tissues can be brought to a new energy state. This is a revolutionary new way of treating nerves, muscle pain, brain injury and other conditions.

Our bodies have an energy information highway that supersedes and drives the chemistry. This is the Inner Physician at work. When we drown the cells of the body with a pharmaceutical drug in the treatment of an ailment there are always side effects and toxicity, because it is interrupting the natural rhythm of the body. The good news is that we are beginning to understand the priority of energy medicine to our health and this is why I am so excited about accessing the Inner Physician in healing.

As I mentioned in an earlier chapter, my first treatment was powerful. It felt like my brain was way too big for my skull and I felt like it was going to explode. I also felt sick to my stomach. My doctor had to drive me home I was so disoriented. When I felt that feeling I realized it wasn't the first time I had a concussion. I had felt that same sick feeling in two previous falls and all three of them were connected; I knew that the current concussion was probably a blessing in disguise because the giant needed to be awakened. My brain had adjusted to the damage from the first two and I wasn't even aware of it. The FSM had brought it into my awareness.

As is always the case with physical issues, this one did indeed turn out to be a blessing in a lot of ways. First I needed to break the pattern of thinking and dissecting everything if I was going to be a master at using the Law of Attraction and manifesting the life I desire. Most of us were taught to plan, set goals and write out all of the details and this doesn't leave room for the magic of the Universe to happen. When I planned and set goals in great detail I met with a lot of resistance because I couldn't see how the magic could happen. I would get caught up in the details, and get in my own way. You can't see expanded possibilities when you are caught up in the details. The Universe can't work when we are planning and scheming, sorry to break it to you.

Our innate nature is one of letting go, trusting and believing in the magic and grace of the Universe. Our natural understanding of dreaming and manifesting is programmed out of us as children, replaced with a program of control, goal setting and action. We lose the sense of magic we had as children through socialization and spend a majority of our life becoming conscious and returning to that place.

The new concussion caused problems with my memory, and it was work to try to organize things in my head and plan. I felt exhausted with how hard it was to retrieve information. It takes 28 days to change a behavior and create a new one and I was having problems with my memory for over a month. I had to find another way to navigate the world. The whack on my head was allowing me to drop into my heart and see the world from that perspective.

Navigating from the heart is the feminine way. Healing comes from the feminine place of receptivity and allowing. As I entered my fourth week of concussion, magical things were beginning to happen. I realized one morning that a concussion usually "knocks you unconscious," and though I wasn't knocked unconscious some of my consciousness was knocked out of my reach. I didn't realize it at the time but parts of my consciousness had been put to sleep through the series of concussions.

As the concussion was leaving my brain I felt my consciousness opening back up and expanding to new levels. I feel like I have come to a new dimension of thinking. I also see why it has been hard for me to focus and hold intentions and I am seeing how easy it is to do so now. It is like waking up from a nap that I didn't know I had taken.

A second component to any trauma is Post-Traumatic Stress Disorder (PTSD). Part of the microcurrent treatment is focused on releasing PTSD. That protocol resulted in interesting dreams all the way back to childhood and traumas experienced at that time. Post-Traumatic Stress Disorder can hinder you from changing beliefs because much of the trauma is cellular and you can't discover it consciously, so I was grateful this process was not uncovering those hidden traumas.

The first day that I used the protocol for PTSD I had a dream that my mother was killed in a small engine plane crash right outside my house. The debris was all over the neighborhood. In the dream the propeller spun around outside my window waking me up. I went out and found only her shoes and a pin she used to wear but no body. Kids were picking things up and I told them to leave them but the sound of my words wouldn't come out. I felt helpless. I was just starting to call the police when I woke up from the dream.

I did some research to understand the dream metaphor and what I found was this: "To dream about a plane crash means something out of your control that you should have been able to trust in has gone haywire. This isn't about you and something you should have been able to do properly. It is about someone or something else that you 'trusted' that let you down completely, in a way that had a huge impact on your life."

This is so profound because when I was four years old I had a seizure from a very high temperature. I was hospitalized and at the time placed in a straightjacket. I was in the hospital for 4 days and the only person I needed was my mother. That is who we seek for comfort developmentally at that age. As I mentioned previously, my mother never visited me in the hospital. This was a traumatic event that changed the course of my life and my ability to trust. It was as if, from that point on, I had made an unconscious commitment to myself to be independent and do everything for myself because I couldn't trust anyone.

Though I had worked on this issue on the emotional and spiritual levels this was still trapped in my cellular memory and still impacting me. I feel like the micro current program for PTSD released it through this dream. If I hadn't had the accident this wouldn't have been uncovered.

I am grateful for the accident that caused the concussion that has led to getting treatment for 2 other concussions that I didn't know I had and waking the sleeping giant. I am grateful for the new unfolding consciousness that is waking in me and excited to see what comes next.

While I was editing this chapter I made a typo that was very informative. I pay attention to those things because I feel like the Universe it trying to get my attention. This is something to remember as you go through your healing process because those little "mistakes" can have a big impact on your healing progress.

Here is the typo:

It was as id, from that point on, I had made an unconscious commitment to myself to be independent and do everything for myself because I couldn't trust anyone.

I saw it right away and went back and corrected it but couldn't help but want to look up the definition of id. Here is the definition (from Kendra Cherry's The Everything Psychology Book):

Definition:

According to Sigmund Freud's psychoanalytic theory of personality, the id is the personality component made up of unconscious psychic energy that works to satisfy basic urges, needs, and desires. The id operates based on the pleasure principle, which demands immediate gratification of needs.

The id is the only part of personality that is present at birth. Freud also suggested that this primitive component of personality existed completely within the unconscious. The id acts as the driving force behind personality. It not only strives to fulfill our most basic urges, many of which are tied directly to survival, it also provides all of the energy necessary to drive personality.

During infancy, before the other components of personality begin to form, children are ruled entirely by the id. Satisfying basic needs for food, drink, and comfort are of the utmost importance. As we grow older, it would obviously be quite problematic if we acted out to satisfy the needs of the id whenever we felt an urge, need, or desire. Fortunately, the other components of personality develop as we age, allowing us to control the demands of the id and behave in socially acceptable ways.

When we are unable to immediately satisfy a need, tension results. The id relies on the primary process to temporarily relieve the tension. The primary process involves creating a mental image either through daydreaming, fantasizing, hallucinating, or some other process.

This is a whole new insight into what might have happened during my hospital stay and perceived abandonment by my mother. It also affirms the conclusion that I came to and why it has caused me problems all of my life. It was an id-driven decision and it makes sense that I would come to the conclusion that I couldn't trust anyone but myself to meet my needs. I made something up to alleviate the tension. I didn't have the ego or superego to modify that decision because they were not yet formed in my personality.

You see why I pay attention to typos and all the other nudges from the Universe!

Let's explore Dreaming for techniques on how to use dreams to discover wellness.

CREATIVE TECHNIQUE
FOR WELLNESS

Dreaming Wellness

"Without leaps of imagination, or dreaming, we lose the excitement of possibilities. Dreaming, after all, is a form of planning."

Gloria Steinem

My Inner Physician comes to me often in my dreams because it knows that this is a place where I completely let go of control and listen. Dreams are a powerful vehicle for healing and I share the following dream, an example of the intense emotions of the dream state, to illustrate that point.

Dream:

> *I was staying with friends who lived in New Mexico. One morning I walked into the kitchen barefoot and got stung by a scorpion. My body began to go numb and I panicked as the poison ran through me. I asked several people in the house to help me but no one responded. It was as if I were invisible. I found the phone and called 911 and I was told not to get quiet until help could get there because it would help my body stay alive if I was active. My fear increased as more of my body went numb. I called out for help but no one came. I was paralyzed from the tip of my nose all the way to my feet. A man came into the room and grabbed me as he changed from black to white. He had a syringe in his hand which he plunged into my heart and released the medicine. I passed out. When I came to a few minutes later I saw him just long enough to get a clear image of who he was, and then I woke up.*

The vivid imagery, body sensations and emotions I felt in the dream made it easy to remember it when I woke up. I thought of it as an initiation dream, where I was at death's doorway and I survived and was gifted with the medicine of scorpion. When I was looking through my journals for dreams for this chapter I discovered another scorpion dream that I had five months earlier, which I had forgotten.

Dream:

> *I was in a brick room with a man who was a gifted artist. He reached down and picked up something and put it in my hair and left me alone in the room. I reached up and discovered a black scorpion, which stung me in the hand as I tossed it away. My first finger was numb where I had been stung and I was afraid it would stay that way and I would never paint again. I was angry and went to find the man to ask him why he had done that. He replied, "I wanted to see how you would respond to an initiation and you did well."*

It is said that repetitive dreams have a message that is important and it repeats itself so that you don't miss the message. I missed this one the first time around so it came again. I have been at death's doorway a number of times in this lifetime and survived and have received powerful medicine in the process. The dream was bring to the surface things that I needed to remember. Here in the dream was an echo of my fear that I would lose my ability to paint. Like the dreams, each of my illnesses had been initiations for me and in retrospect I can see that I did very well.

Dreams offer us an opportunity to observe and experience the spirit of creativity in action without the restriction of third dimensional density. Like an artist in the studio we can cut, paste and move image as though creating a collage and what is revealed can shock and surprise us to attention. In this way the dream becomes a laboratory for creative problem solving, and answers to questions that don't come easily in our waking life surface easily. We can find the cause of our illnesses and ask the dream to give us solutions. Our dreams can act as oracles that are directly connected to our Inner Physician.

By the time a person reaches the age of 75 they have slept 25 years and dreamed for 10 of them. I imagine the time spent in daydreaming is somewhat similar. If 10 years of our life is spent dreaming, it would be good to know what is happening while we dream and discover ways to use the information. Dreams appear to be random images that come to us without our control and we can learn to have more control by becoming conscious in our dreams. We can learn to recall our dreams, incubate answers to questions and be lucid in our dreaming.

Ancient civilizations were well aware of the benefits of dream incubation as a source of guidance and the importance and power of dreams is well established. Dreams are a powerful problem-solving agent because the conscious mind can't access all the information that the unconscious mind can while dreaming. From the temples of antiquity to the sleep labs of modern days, humans have tried to understand and explain their dreams and apply them in the waking state.

Dreams have influenced the decisions of world leaders, have given insights to world-changing scientists and have inspired gifted artists with creative inspiration. The first known record of dreams was made by a king in Mesopotamia over 5000 years ago. They were the first people to use dream incubation, which is to think of a problem, ask a question and have it answered in the dream. The Mesopotamians had specific rituals they followed to prepare for dream incubation, done only by a priest, which included special songs and prayers. They also had a special place for the incubation to take place. Greek dream incubation temples still exist today and it is still possible to sleep in them. Wouldn't that be an interesting experience?

Dreams have a history of being used for medical diagnosis and treatment. The Greeks dream temples were also used to access healing dreams, as well as incubation dreams.

The ancient Egyptians created Serapeums, which were temples used for incubation named after the God of dreams, Serapis. These Serapeums were so popular that they were erected throughout Egypt and the Middle East. Each temple had a priest who was an expert on dreams who helped in the dream preparations. The person who wanted to incubate a dream would stay in the temple and undergo several days of various rituals of cleansing, fasting, purging, abstinence from sex, making offerings, and praying before they would go to sleep in the incubation chamber to receive the dream. People could also send a surrogate to dream for them.

The Greek God Asklepios, who was known to be a magician of dreams, would often appear to the dreamer in a visionary dream, perform a symbolic operation, and the seeker would awaken either healed or with specific guidance about their concern. He inspired dreams that could then be interpreted. It was believed that dreams were seen as an important means of therapy, a fact that is essential for understanding the meaning of the Serapeum. In ancient times dreams were associated with healing and medicine. They continue to be seen that way today. It gives me some comfort to think that an angel helped me heal my gallbladder and maybe it was Asklepios who assisted them. In our dreams anything is possible, right?

Philosophers Sigmund Freud and Carl Jung resurrected the use of dreams in healing by incorporating them into their clinical work with clients. Jung believed that the deeper layer of unconscious, which he calls the collective unconscious, is an inborn and universal part of the unconscious identical in all people. Jung thought that dreams could help us grow and heal through use of archetypes which are symbols of life processes. Jung said, "The archetype is ... an inherited tendency of the human mind to form representations of mythological motifs –

representations that vary a great deal without losing their basic pattern." Jung proposed that these symbols are mental images from the collective unconscious, which help us to recognize and integrate the parts of ourselves that we have disowned or are apprehensive about. We can work with our dreams as though they were oracles, just like ancient man had done, to access information to questions that stump us in waking life. With practice and routine recording of dreams we will enhance our ability to remember and understand our dreams.

I read a quote by Deepak Chopra that has always stuck with me. "What if you slept, and what if, in your sleep you dreamed? And what if, in your dream, you went to heaven and there plucked a strange and beautiful flower? And what if, when you awoke, you had the flower in your hand? What then?" What if what we dreamed became reality as if plucked from the garden of God? What would you do if you woke from a dream and found the dream object lying on your pillow next to you? What if you awoke from a dream and were cured of your illness like I was? The dream landscape is unexplainable and seemingly magical and it provides us with valuable information. Dreaming may occur in both waking and sleeping consciousness and we always have access to it. Inspiration, psychic and intuitive information and AH moments come from the dream landscape.

I think that the beauty and power of the dream landscape is that we have little control of it when we are in it, unless we learn the technique of lucid dreaming. In the dream an environment for healing can be created and we just become a part of it. Because it is a dream we don't question the magical things that are happening like we do in waking reality. We don't try to stop it or ignore it, we are a part of it. And if an angel walks into our dream we welcome them fearlessly like we would an old friend. I don't know about you but if an angel or giant being walked into my bedroom when I was awake I don't think I would be quite as fearless. In dreams we allow healing to happen and if we do we can return from the dream with the dream reality becoming part of our waking reality.

When we slip into our dreams we experience a time of complete rest in the familiar blackness as we float freely in consciousness. As we float in the medium of dreams we are in direct contact with all potential energy and all possibilities. In waking and sleeping dreams we cross the borders of time and space into no time and retrieve information that we bring back to ordinary reality where time, space and timing are the medium of life. The language of dreams is different from our everyday language and is hard to put into words and why we often forget our dreams upon waking. Dreaming in the Yaqui tradition, from the Aztecs of Mexico, is considered an act of encountering parallel Universes in the realms of potential that exists on a

Dream Weave. A dream exists beyond language and by the time you put words and descriptions on it you are already several generations removed from the actual experience. The experience of a dream is primal, preverbal, pre-sensual, other-worldly and incomparable.

If we approach the dream as a vehicle for exploring potential we can gather useful information about our path. If we get caught up in analyzing the dream from the perspective of discovering shadow (that part, according to Jung, that we have not owned) we might miss useful information. Every time we return to ordinary consciousness from dreaming we awaken changed as if by chance we have brought that beautiful flower back with us. Our dreams are the realm of our Inner Physician.

AWAKENING YOUR INNER PHYSICIAN

We can use our dreams as an oracle by using a technique called dream incubation, which is asking the dream world to give you specific information about a question or project you want to manifest. In the case of your health and wellness you can ask the dream question specifically to your Inner Physician. Before you go to sleep, hold the question in your mind and in the dream you will find your answer.

You could ask to be shown the path to wellness. Always remember to ask that you remember your dream and be prepared with paper and pen by your bed so you can write when you wake up. Dream recall is an important part of the incubation process and its benefits are significantly enhanced with intention, practice and focus. Making a consistent effort to remember and record your dreams will help your waking mind ally itself more closely with your dream experience. This will also increase your imagination and intuitive capabilities, which are crucial to connecting with your Inner Physician. A dream journal next to your bed with a pen and a small flashlight will assist in this process.

In the beginning was the dream of the Great Dreamer (God/Source/ Creator) and from it our world was created. How many dreams have we carried since we were young that have yet to materialize? That is because they are waiting for the time and timing of this reality to catch up and align with no time from which they came. Often it takes a lot of patience on the part of the dreamer to continue to nurture a dream until it comes into physical reality. Do you have dreams you have carried for years, knowing someday, somehow they will become reality? Keep nurturing them; they may be right around the next corner waiting for you to walk into them.

To incubate a dream, sit on the side of your bed and quiet yourself. When your body and mind feel quiet lie down and hold a question clearly in your mind for a few minutes. As you prepare to go to sleep ask yourself to clearly remember a dream that reveals the answer as an insight, an actual experience or both. As you fall asleep, keep the question in your mind, trusting that the exercise will be successful. If other thoughts distract you, just return to your incubation focus.

Before you fall off to sleep tonight ask your dreaming self to answer a question about your current health concern and ask to remember it when you wake up. You can ask to connect to your Inner Physician for direct guidance into your issue. The moment you awaken, whether in the morning or during the night, record any dreams or thoughts that you are having. Maybe it is just one word, or a sentence or image. Jot it down so you can think about it and/or research it in the morning. Without judgment or censorship record what you remember in the morning reflecting on any dreams and thoughts that you recorded, making whatever associations, interpretations and waking life connections you can. The answer may or may not be obvious but trust that the process is working. If you get insights try to put them into practice in your life and watch what happens. Even if you don't recall the dream your incubation may be simmering in the unconscious and may result in a sudden flash of revelation or insight during the day. Continue to do this incubation process each night until you fell complete with the information. If you maintain an attitude of gratitude for the guidance you receive it will promote further insights and future success in dream incubation. Our dreams are the best storytellers, and through their stories the deepest healing can occur.

Personally I find that when I start a dream incubation process I will get answers in the dream but also flashes of inspiration of things I can do to support my healing. It could be that a specific herb, a crystal or kind of food pops into your head and when you look up what it is for it turns out to be perfect for your particular affliction. You can recognize inspiration from the Inner Physician because it comes like flashes from out of nowhere. Pay attention, it could be the answer to your prayer!

"I've dreamt in my life dreams that have stayed with me ever after, and changed my ideas: they've gone through and through me, like wine through water, and altered the color of my mind." Emily Bronte

CHAPTER TWELVE

The Phoenix Rises

"Change is the constant, the signal for rebirth, the egg of the phoenix."

Christina Baldwin

"The phoenix hope, can wing her way through the desert skies, and still defying fortune's spite: revive from the ashes and rise."

Miguel de Cervantes

It has taken me 9 years to write this book and almost 4 to get back to it and write this chapter. I had to work through a lot of resistance before I could bring this book into the world but the story in this chapter is another reason I had to wait. This is the story that brings me full circle.

One of the best ways to support health and wellness is by giving your body the proper nutrition. When our body has the nutrients it needs the Inner Physician can do what it needs to do to bring our bodies back into balance. I have spent years studying nutrition and searching out the purest supplements to put into my body to support wellness. In talking about supplementation it is important to know that each person is different and their bodies have different needs, so when I talk about what has worked for me keep this in mind. Because of the FDA regulations, companies that sell supplements cannot say their products will cure or relieve symptoms from any disease. Knowing what I know about nutrition I always believe it is worth a shot especially when the supplements are all food based.

This is a story about my intestinal issue, which I wrote about earlier, and how the addition of proper nutrition and supplements changed everything. I believe it was a miracle! I am sharing this as an example of what happened to me because I gave my body proper nutrition.

We all have parts of our body that we don't like; mine is my stomach. I should clarify that. I don't like the way it looks, and have been working for a long time to get to the place where I like it more. But the way it looks is because of the life-saving surgery, which took place 29 years ago, when I had a strangulated bowel. I talked about that in an earlier chapter and this is why I feel I have come full circle. That event started me on my journey of awakening, 29 years ago, and now that event brings me to a new place.

I have an 8-inch scar going from the top to the bottom of my abdomen that I have always been embarrassed by. It has looked like a second butt when I have carried too much weight. When they removed the two feet of intestine they also removed two specific functions: the absorption of B12 and the absorption of bile. Because I could no longer absorb them I had to have B12 injections and take a medication that would absorb bile so I didn't get sick.

If I didn't take the medicine I would get bile salts diarrhea. I hadn't had a normal bowel movement in 25 years and often got sick even if I took the medication. I tried several times over the years to stop taking it, because it is a pain, it tastes nasty and it is expensive, but I never could without getting sick. I was afraid to be without it, actually because I knew what the consequences were. I always needed to know where the restroom was wherever I went in case of an emergency.

Here is where the beautiful miracle part comes in, and where my personal phoenix rises from the ashes....

I was part of an 8-week challenge with It Works! Global to test a new protein powder/super food that they were going to introduce to the line called Ultimate ProFIT. I was excited about this product because I had used a lot of different protein powders in the past but none with the quality ingredients this one had. I love the fact that the protein is from a whey powder that comes from grass-fed cows and is processed in such a way that all the nutrition is intact. I also like that there is a small amount of soy that is from non-GMO sources. People get confused because there is so much controversy around soy but it is really Genetic Modification that causes the problems. Along with that it contains superfoods, good quality fiber and is sweetened with Stevia. It was a winner as far as I am concerned and I couldn't wait to try it.

The first time I mixed it up and drank it I could feel the life force in this product. I had never felt that before and I knew I was giving my body something that was going to have a positive impact on it.

A few weeks into the challenge using ProFIT I started feeling constipated, which had never been my experience in the past. Three weeks into the challenge I decided to stop taking the bile medication and see what would happen.

After taking two particular products (ProFIT and one called Greens) for three months I started wondering what if anything it had done in my body. I wanted to be able to share a story with people about why I thought these were such great products. Suddenly I realized that I was no longer having problems with my bowel. The issue that I had been dealing with for 25 years was gone. It is not uncommon that a problem heals and we don't realize it because there is no longer anything drawing attention to the problem and it usually happens gradually over time. I was shocked!

Not only was my intestinal tract back to normal but my allergies to wheat and dairy were gone too. If your intestinal tract is healthy the body will be healthy too. Allergies are common in people who have intestinal dysfunction. I found I had increased energy, improved sleep and I was able to make shifts emotionally and spiritually, with ease.

Now, you tell me how your body can recreate a function that was removed, because I can't figure it out. That is how beautiful our bodies are. This was life changing for me! I never thought I would ever get off of the medication and have a normal body again. So what if my stomach has a large crater through it? When you think about it on the level of renewal and what some call healing, it is beautiful even in the state it is in.

I asked the formulator of the ProFIT if she thought it was possible that this happened because I was taking it. She said it was the combination of ProFIT and the Greens, which were part of the Ultimate Makeover that I was testing. My body got the nutrition that it needed and it somehow came

304

back into balance so I now have normal bowel function. Proper nutrition can do this! That was 4 years ago and my bowels are still functioning as they should.

I was happy to be alive after having surgery and was willing to live with the results of having my intestine removed. I never dreamed I would ever experience normal bowel function again! I love miracles, especially when they happen to me.

To learn more about the Ultimate Makeover and ProFIT see the resource section in the back of the book on the page about Your Body Ecologist.

CREATIVE TECHNIQUE FOR WELLNESS

Wellness from the Inside out

"The body cannot be cured without regard for the soul."

Socrates

"True healing is found in the memory of wholeness."

Deepak Chopra

"In a healthy person a state of equilibrium exists between the physical, mental, emotional and spiritual bodies. In illness, an imbalance occurs which results in discomfort and eventually disease."

"Illness or pain is just an extension of negative emotion. When you are no longer feeling any resistance to it, it's a non-issue."

Abraham-Hicks

"Any illness is a direct message to you that tells you how you have not been loving who you are, cherishing yourself in order to be who you are. This is the basis of all healing."

Barbara Brennan

In earlier times, physicians considered a patient's spiritual condition of equal importance to the physical state in the healing process. Western medicine is just beginning to wake up to the idea of a holistic approach to healing and alternative medicines. I call that spiritual consciousness the Inner Physician. I hope someday it is commonplace.

Each healing crisis that I went through gave me more awareness of who I truly am. Every time I was able to discover the lesson that my illness presented me with, the more conscious I became. There are all kinds of ways to become more conscious; I happened to have had a lot of physical issues that were on my path, not just the normal ones people have. I went from being one of the most negative people on the planet, after my divorce, to a person who trusts myself and the wisdom of my body and who is creating a positive reality for myself. It wasn't easy and I had to do it one thought at a time and one moment at a time.

I remember vividly the day I decided I didn't want to live in a negative mindset any longer. I made a commitment to start finding positive things to focus on. It took me several days to find the first positive thing, and several days after that to find another. I started finding more and more positive things happening in my life and one day everything shifted and I was focused more on the positive and less on the negative. These days I barely put much energy into negative thinking.

True and lasting healing comes from the inside out. What I mean is that when we line up with being healthy and start doing things and thinking things that support health in the body, our body automatically heals. It can't be any other way. We are in partnership with our bodies and our responsibility in the partnership is to nurture and feed our bodies with the best food possible so it can do its part most efficiently. When we realize that our body has a consciousness for wellness, which is our natural healthy state, and that we are co-creating with something higher, our consciousness changes. As our consciousness changes we make different choices about what we put in our body.

If you think about it our bodies are made up of millions of cells and new cells are created every minute. If our body created unhealthy cells it can create healthy ones to replace them if we give the cells the right nourishment. We can go from a state of disease to a state of health over time by changing the way we feed our body. Our body has innate intelligence and if we give it what it needs it will come back into balance and vibrant health.

We are also responsible for keeping it strong and flexible through some form of exercise or movement. I can't use the excuse that I don't have the time, because if I get sick because I haven't taken care of my body, the choice to take time to heal won't be mine. I will be forced to take the time. We are living longer as a species than ever before and if we maintain our part in the partnership agreement we can live a long, healthy, youthful life. If we make a commitment to be healthy, strong and conscious the Universe will step in to support us.

Two of my favorite authors, Esther and Jerry Hicks, give a great description of the energy that I call the Inner Physician. They say, "You see, your bodies are made up of trillions of cells, each holding the vision of their perfection and of their perfect place in the perfect whole....You see... every time anyone, even a tiny little cell in your body, asks for something – it is always given. So, when a body is injured, in some way, the cells closest to the injury calculate exactly what they need to regain their balance – and they send out immediate requests. And, instantly, the Energy begins to flow, and all other aspects of the body being to respond, too. Special helping nutrients of all kinds begin making their way through the body, and the natural healing begins, immediately. And when the person, who lives in this body, is happy or eager, or appreciative – then the healing is allowed. But if that person is sad or angry, or fearful – the healing is hindered or resisted."

It is my experience that the body responds to the thoughts we offer it. Every time I have had a physical experience of disharmony and changed my focus to harmony and health, my body was able to return to health and harmony, even when I was told that it wasn't possible. Even though it was hard for me to believe at first, I have learned that we need to start where we are and move to the next highest thought until we get to our goal of wellness. If we are feeling depressed moving to anger about our illness would be moving up the scale because there is energy in anger. If we want to experience wellness we must stop defending against illness and give our attention to wellness. I see so many people who are sick say things like, "I am going to fight this!" What we fight against persists. What we embrace and accept can transform.

The good news, and the bad news, is: we create our own experience with our thoughts. It is bad news because this core philosophical principle is not the cultural thought system that we have been imprinted with and educated from. Think of what the world would be like if we had come from a philosophy of abundance right from the beginning. What if we were raised to believe that anything is possible? The problem is that we have been socialized for the most part to worry about what we don't want rather than to focus all of our energy on what we do want. The truth is the Universe manifests what we imagine and think about whether it is by default or deliberate creation. The good news is we can learn how to use the operating principles of the Universe right now and if we don't like our present reality we can change our thoughts immediately and begin to create the life we desire. It isn't easy because that hasn't been our program but it can be done.

In every moment that you think about something other than illness, you are stopping the illness from going forward. We

311

have to be motivated to try something new. From there we can move to hope and so on. We come into health and wellness by bringing our vibration into alignment with health and wellness, one thought at a time, from the inside out.

When we change our inner environment our outer environment has to change too.

Bringing our body back into balance after disease requires us to take the soul's journey of discovering who we truly are. I believe that knowing our authentic self is one of the reasons we are here on earth in the first place. It is a journey of discovering lost parts of the self and integrating them.

Searching for my truth, I realized what a gift it is to be alive, to feel the sun on my face and the wind blowing through my hair. Every time I had a healing crisis my soul led me on a journey of self-discovery. Each time I made a commitment to be well, the forces within me could mobilize my energies toward coming back into balance. When I trusted my Inner Physician I was led where I needed to go; whether it was within myself or through seeking outside help, the path opened up. Wellness resources abound, both inside us and all around us. When it comes down to it, health happens inside us and is not done by some outside force. If we align ourselves with health and wellness and go about the task of creating a healthy inner environment the only thing that can happen is coming back into balance.

Healing has been defined as "the process of bringing together aspects of one's self, body-mind-spirit, at deeper levels of inner knowing, leading toward integration and balance with each aspect having equal importance and value." Sometimes in order to get to this deep level of inner knowing we need to experience a crisis. For me, it seemed as though I often didn't hear the message in the past when it came in other forms. I choose not to learn my lessons by going into a healing crisis any more. Now I choose to think thoughts and feel feelings that support having a healthy body every day. Western medical science has pursued a path of fragmentation, separating mind from body, thought from emotion, and organ from organ. This has produced many marvelous technologies for symptom removal. But it does not produce healing. Healing involves reintegrating or remembering and bringing all the lost parts of us back together. That is the journey to wholeness and the path to the authentic self.

AWAKENING YOUR INNER PHYSICIAN

Now take a moment, and feel the healing energy that surrounds you. There is a universal stream of healing energy that surrounds each of us in every moment with divine guidance and Love. It is the same universal stream of healing that is connected to the Inner Physician who is waiting for a word from you to step in and make things right in your body. Be still, move from your head into your heart and feel your heart opening to receive this Love. All it takes from you is to open up and let it in. Know that you are deeply loved by the Loving Creator who made us all and of which we are still a part. Let the Love surround and embrace you. Feel the loving arms holding you as you let go.

Take a deep breath, release disharmony and breathe in harmony. Let this source of Love fill you. Let it fill your cells with healthy life force energy and let it help you release the cells that are not in harmony with that intention. It is healing you in this very moment.

Yes, that's right, you are healing right here and right now. See yourself as perfectly healed. You have stepped onto the path to recovery and your body is moving toward its natural state which is health and wellness. Open to the voice of your Inner Physician, let go and step aside and listen deeply, so that it can do what it does best, keeping your body in perfect health. From this moment forward you are on the path of perfect health and wellness. And so it is....

CHAPTER THIRTEEN

Coming Full Circle

"Time is a companion that goes with us on a journey. It reminds us to cherish each moment, because it will never come again. What we leave behind is not as important as how we have lived."

Captain Jean-Luc Picard

True health insurance is not something we pay a monthly premium on so our bills are covered when we get sick, it is giving our body what it needs to stay healthy on a daily basis. Whether you are fighting fatigue, looking for ways to boost your immune system or recover from illness, prevention and management of symptoms is often helped significantly by the foods we eat. When the body gets the nutrition it needs the Inner Physician can do what it needs to do to bring your body back into balance. There are many books written about specific diets and foods to eat to support regaining your health so I won't go into foods here except to say that in the past we were able to get all the vitamins and minerals from fruits and vegetables, meat and fish. Now most modern fruits and vegetables are grown to increase their sugar content, not their nutritional value. As a result, most fruits and vegetables are artificially high in fructose and sugars and lower in key nutrients. Our soil is also depleted of important minerals so they aren't found in foods we eat any more. Animals and some plants are being loaded with growth hormones so they will grow faster and this is wreaking havoc on our bodies. The internal environment that is created by these foods is not conducive to health and wellness. This chapter is just to get you started in thinking about looking at ways to eat more nutritiously.

Ideally, we should be consuming our vitamins and minerals through foods in their whole, natural and organic form with all the essential co-factors and enzymes essential for delivering the nutrients directly to our cells. Due to the state of our soils and planet, food is unlikely to always provide the essential vitamins and minerals required for optimal health. That is why we need to supplement our diets with vitamins and minerals. The best supplements are ones made from whole food sources rather than synthetic materials.

We are now faced with so many things that impede our health, from stress and busy lifestyles, to genetically modified foods and chemical pollutants, and more of us are developing food allergies. Before processed foods people were able to get what they needed from their food. That is not true any longer. Not all processed foods are bad but many are because of the addition of sodium, preservatives and MSG. We are all being impacted by the over-processing of foods.

People often complain about how much nutritional supplements cost, when in reality it costs much less to supplement your diet with the things that are missing than to let your body fall into a state of disease that can result in huge medical bills later. If we give our body the food it needs to maintain homeostasis and create healthy cells we are less likely to get sick in the first place.

I remember learning about the food pyramid and the four food groups when I was in grade school but that was as far as it went. I didn't learn much about good nutrition from my parents; in fact my mother had seven meals that she made, one for each day of the week. We were never encouraged to drink water and water wasn't part of our daily regimen so I never developed a habit of drinking enough of it. Fast food was just being introduced and everyone was eating it. No one knew how harmful it would turn out to be. I grew up in the age of Twinkies and Big Mac's. Becoming a conscious eater was a process that took me years to establish as I learned through trial and error what was good for me and what was not and at the same time was continually bombarded with food propaganda by the media.

One of the things that became clear to me during my discovery of my Inner Physician was the importance of good nutrition. I spent a lot of time looking for nutritional supplements that would impact at the cellular level because I knew that if I could give my cells what they needed they could create healthy cells and any disorder in the body could heal itself. I looked for supplements that were bioavailable at the cell level and easily absorbed. You will find the company where I buy my supplements in the resources in the back of the book.

Without adequate supplementation, the normal functioning of cells often becomes impaired, resulting in poor health. Pollution, oxidation, contamination, refined foods, stress, and dozens of other health hazards assault the body's trillions of cells. Many of the "symptoms" of disease are in fact the body crying out for nutritional support, because cellular health is based on nutrient synergy and the optimal daily intake and assimilation of vitamins and other essential nutrients.

I have spent many years improving my nutrition so that I was eating very healthily, because a healthy body is an environment where disease can't live. Seventy percent of our immune system is in our intestine and because of my surgery my intestinal tract was highly susceptible to problems. I knew I wanted to find things that would support a healthy intestinal tract because that would improve my immune system. I have found several products that have changed the condition of my intestinal tract and almost removed all of my allergies. They have been created with the highest quality, natural ingredients that are supporting people around the world to come back to health and wellness. In this chapter I will talk about how they have impacted me.

Over the past several years I have done a lot of research into finding the highest quality nutritional supplements to take and have found several companies using cutting-edge technology to deliver the best benefits. When I started taking supplements that focused on relieving stress and giving the DNA the food it needed my body responded in a resounding "yes."

One of the biggest causes of disease aside from poor diet is stress. Before you can unlock the code and come into harmony in your body you must relieve your body of stress, which is at the root of the disease process. It can show up in many forms such as insomnia, depression, anxiety, headache, poor digestion, irritability, immune disturbances, hormonal imbalances, or fatigue. In extreme cases it can cause conditions such as angina, asthma, autoimmune disease, cancer, cardiovascular disease, the common cold, depression, diabetes type II, headaches, hypertension, immune suppression and imbalance, IBS, PMS, irregular menstruation, rheumatoid arthritis, ulcerative colitis, ulcers, thyroid problems and many others.

The body exists in homeostasis, which means it is in a balance that works in harmony physically, mentally and emotionally. Stress can be defined as anything that "pushes" the body away from homeostasis. A certain amount of that is good since it increases growth and adaptability. Exercise causes stress that is good for your body unless it is done to the extreme. Severe stress or prolonged stress can damage the system, pushing it beyond its ability to adapt.

Stress can come from many sources ranging from bad diet, toxins, pathogens, and genetic weakness to a nervous system locked into a hypervigilant state due to trauma. Persistent nervous stress ultimately affects the autonomic nervous system which affects brain waves and hormone output. When our ancestors experienced stress it only lasted for brief periods of time usually resulted from a life-threatening emergency. We live in a world that is full of stress whether it is rush-hour traffic, the news on TV, pollution or the job.

Stress is all around us all of the time and it is often occurring in our bodies and we aren't aware of it because we have become accustomed to it.

Stress causes an imbalance in the hormonal systems of the body. The body releases the hormone cortisol under stress. Cortisol has certain brief benefits but those benefits become liabilities when experienced for a longer term as they usually are in modern life. Excess Cortisol is toxic and it usually settles around the midsection of the body as fat. As we age this hormone is overproduced and stays in the body longer. In excess it throws homeostasis out of balance and suppresses the immune system. Over time this wears on the body. You will learn techniques for reducing your stress later in the book, but here I want to address the nutritional component of stress.

Along with supplements it is important to develop conscious eating habits if we want to maintain health and wellness. Conscious eating is making healthy choices about what we eat. It also means relaxing the mind and body before we eat so we slow down the process and don't overeat. Eating on the run is not only hard on the body but we usually make poor choices of what to eat when we are in a hurry.

Remember to listen to your body. Follow the wisdom inherent in your own body to guide you to healthy food choices. Use discrimination when eating and try to choose organic, whole, natural foods whenever possible. Eat when you feel a natural hunger in your body. We have been trained to eat three meals a day, such as at 7 AM, 12 PM and 5 PM, and those might not be the best times for your particular body. Some people actually do better on six small meals scattered throughout the day. Be aware of your unconscious motivations when eating and make sure you are eating to satisfy the physical need of the body, not an emotional need.

Finally we have a responsibility to our body to focus our attention and thoughts on health. Our positive thoughts can impact our health and wellness on many levels. Our challenge is to believe in our health and in the power of our bodies to heal. How many commercials to we see on TV that are promoting medication that will heal this or that condition? I am sure you have heard the disclaimers as well, the ones that say taking this product may produce side effects such as heart irregularities, difficulties in breathing, profuse vomiting or sudden death, and if any of these conditions occur consult your doctor immediately. Have you ever noticed that those conditions are said very rapidly so that you don't pay attention?

Medicine is not a perfect science and doctors do not know everything. It concerns me that we have been taught to look up to our doctors as the experts and do exactly what they say, even when we might have an inner feeling to do something else. I think staying healthy is a balance between sound medical advice and really tuning in to the deep wisdom of our bodies. The messages on TV can cause us to worry and place our focus on disease and where we place our focus is what gets created. It is impossible to stay healthy thinking about disease, the bird flu or the next cure-all for such and such a problem.

As you develop healthy eating habits and begin to eat healthy foods you will notice incredible health benefits. Honor yourself for the healthy choices you make, incorporate yoga and exercise and conscious eating into your life, and treat your body like the temple that it is. When you add an exercise routine and techniques and supplements for reducing stress your life will change dramatically. There are also deeper rewards that include a heightened awareness of conscious eating and listening to your body, and a deeper and more fulfilling experience of enjoying your food. Your life will be more rewarding as you begin to seek true contentment rather than instant gratification.

My experience changing my diet, using supplements and detoxifying has further supported my body to come back into balance, even though I had a condition that was with me for 25 years. That is how important it is to find the highest quality supplements for your body.

 Check Resources at the back of the book to find out more about the company, It Works! Global, where you can purchase supplements as well as herbal wraps and other products for detoxification of the body and weight-loss and other supportive products.

CREATIVE TECHNIQUE FOR WELLNESS

Eliminating Stress

Relaxing is the best way to eliminate stress and there are many ways to do that. As you read earlier in the chapter, when you eliminate stress it has a big impact on your health and wellness. Stress release is something you want to practice throughout your healing journey. You deserve it, it's good for you, and it takes less time than you think. Many techniques that are good for stress relief have already been discussed throughout the book including breath work, imagery, and visualization. You can get yourself back into a balanced and relaxed state in less than 15 minutes with some techniques.

1. Meditate

We have all heard about the benefits of meditation, but we often avoid it because we are afraid we won't do it right or we don't have time to do it. In reality anything we do can become a meditation from walking, doing the dishes to taking a shower as well as sitting quietly in the traditional manner.

A few minutes of practice a day, of whichever form you choose, can ease anxiety because meditation actually alters the brain chemistry.

Here is a simple sitting meditation. Sit up straight with both feet on the floor. Close your eyes. Focus your attention on reciting – out loud or silently – a positive mantra such as, "I feel at peace," or "I love myself," or "I love my body's ability to heal itself," or "I trust my Inner Physician to heal my body." Place one hand on your belly to synchronize the mantra with your breaths. Let any distracting thoughts float by like clouds as you repeat the mantra you have chosen. Do this until you feel yourself relax.

2. Breathe Deeply

We covered the benefits of the breath in an earlier chapter and how it can be healing to your body. Take a 5-minute break and focus on your breathing. Find a comfortable chair and sit up straight, with your eyes closed and your hand on your belly. It doesn't matter which hand you use. Slowly inhale through your nose, feeling the breath start in your abdomen and work its way to the top of your head. Reverse the process as you exhale through your mouth to calm any emotional arousal. This is what is known as circular breathing. Use this breathing technique whenever you are in a stressful situation and you need to slow down your mental chatter and relax.

3. Exercise

The physical benefits of exercise are well known for improving your physical condition and fighting disease, and physicians encourage patients to be physically active. Exercise can also be vital for maintaining mental fitness and reducing stress.

Scientists have found that regular aerobic exercise decreases overall levels of tension, elevates and stabilizes mood, improves sleep, and improves self-esteem. Even five minutes of aerobic exercise can stimulate anti-anxiety effects.

Exercise and stress management are also closely linked. Exercise provides a distraction from stressful situations, as well as an outlet for frustrations, and gives you a lift via endorphins as well. When stress affects the brain, with its many nerve connections, the rest of the body feels the impact. When your body feels better, so does your mind. Exercise and other physical activity produce endorphins which are chemicals in the brain that act as natural painkillers. They improve your ability to sleep, which also reduces stress.

4. Tune In to Your Body

Mentally scan your body to get a sense how you are being impacted by stress each day. To do this lie on your back, or sit with your feet on the floor. Start at your toes and work your way slowly up to your scalp, noticing how your body feels.

Simply be aware of places you feel tight or loose without trying to change anything. Take a couple of minutes to imagine each deep breath flowing to that body part where you feel tightness. Repeat this process as you move your focus up your body, paying close attention to sensations you feel in each body part. A more complete body scan will be included on the Meditation CD.

5. Do something you really enjoy.

Each day offers the chance to find joy and fulfillment if we can discover activities and hobbies that help us unwind and let loose. When you no longer find interest and enjoyment in what used to make you happy, this is very bad sign. Don't let stress steal your joy.

6. Use visualization to calm your mind.

Sometimes we just need a break from the daily grind but don't have time for a vacation. When you're feeling overwhelmed, close your eyes and visualize yourself on the beach, in the mountains, or wherever you find nourishment and respite. In terms of your health visualize that you are in a calm place and whatever is bothering you is not there for just a few minutes. If you can take your mind off your issue for just a few minutes you will see a reduction in symptoms and pain.

7. Change your environment.

The place and situation you're in has a big impact on how you feel. If there's a conversation or interaction that bothers you, get out of the situation. Go get some fresh air to collect your thoughts. Go for a walk, go sit in the garden, go to a place where you feel centered and get yourself back to balance and out of negative thinking.

8. Drink chamomile tea or any tea that will help you relax.

On the top of the list of fluids with a calming effect is chamomile tea. If you really need something to help you relax, this drink can bring on sleepiness and has a sedating effect.

9. Yoga.

Yoga is one of the oldest self-improvement practices around, dating back over 5 thousand years! It combines the practices of several other stress management techniques such as breathing, meditation, imagery and movement, giving you a lot of benefit for the amount of time and energy required. If you start a daily practice of yoga it will support you through your illness and help you maintain your health and wellbeing beyond. Do some research to learn more about the various forms of yoga and how to use it to manage stress.

10. Laugh more.

We have all heard the saying, "Laughter is the best medicine." A good sense of humor can't cure all ailments, but it can help you feel better, even if you have to force yourself to fake a laugh at first. When you laugh, it not only lightens your mental load but also causes positive physical changes in your body. Laughter fires up and then cools down your stress response. So read some jokes, tell some jokes, watch a comedy or hang out with your funny friends.

AWAKENING YOUR INNER PHYSICIAN

This is by no means an exhaustive list of activities that will reduce stress. Find something that works for you, and it could be a few activities, and create a daily ritual for yourself. If you create a practice that you are doing everyday your stress will be greatly reduced to begin with. You will automatically know what to do to get back into center if you do get out of balance when you get stressed out. This is imperative if you are managing a healing journey. You want to use all of your energy to heal your body and don't want to expend precious energy being stressed out. If you create a ritual for yourself that you do every day your Inner Physician will thank you.

CHAPTER FOURTEEN

Joy and Gratitude ~ The Healing Elixir

"Joy is not dependent on circumstances, it is what bubbles up inside of us when we allow ourselves to recognize how good things really are."

Katelyn Mariah

Since ancient times, philosophers and sages from every spiritual tradition have taught that cultivating gratitude is a key to experiencing deeper levels of happiness, fulfillment, and wellbeing.

One of the fastest ways to empower our body and move toward health and wellness is through an attitude of appreciation and gratitude. What you focus on and appreciate creates more of the same. By concentrating on how much you appreciate your body, no matter what state it is in, the more likely you are to activate miracles. Even when we are not feeling well there is so much about our body that is working and the more you appreciate that, the more you will feel better overall.

Gratitude is an extremely powerful force that we can use to expand our joy, feel more at peace and even improve our health. One of the best ways to impact healing is to cultivate an attitude of gratitude. Gratitude is magnetic and brings more of what we are grateful for to us. Gratitude is a powerful part of the Law of Attraction. It raises your vibration and brings you into harmony with the energy of the Universe. It can immediately transform all areas of your life. When we focus joyfully on what is going right in our world we are activating the magnetics of the Law of Attraction. Gratitude is being aware of the blessings.

In the healing arena we may know that we are not healed but by focusing on the baby steps and giant leaps you are making in that direction you are sending a vibrational signal to the Universe/God/Creator that you appreciate what you have and you will see more of the same manifesting. Being grateful brings you more to be grateful for. It is like magic.

In my own healing journey being grateful would get me out of a funk and refocus me on what I wanted to create. If I paid attention to the little things that were happening, such as being able to move my finger a tiny bit, when I broke my wrist, I started to see the progress I was really making. The more I focused on progress, the more progress I made.

When I tried to have the expectation that I would heal completely when I was in pain and couldn't move, I was filled with doubt that things would ever change. Tony Robbins says, "Trade your expectation for appreciation and the world will change instantly." That is what happened to me when I moved into a place of gratitude. When I could be grateful for the good that was happening and grateful for the fact that I have an inner intelligence that knows how to heal when I get out of the way, healing took place.

Being grateful brings you more to be grateful for. Let's say you are trying to affirm that your body is healthy and in a complete state of wellness, when you are in fact very sick. Your mind naturally drifts back to your perceived lack of wellness. If you stay focused on that you will feel sicker and more hopeless. This is when adopting an attitude of gratitude comes in perfectly.

Instead of trying to affirm something that you don't really believe, start being grateful for what you do have. For example, I am grateful for this wonderful, fluffy pillow that makes me feel more comfortable when I am lying in bed. I am grateful for this lovely cup of tea that is so soothing to my throat. I am grateful for the beautiful flowers my sister sent, that fill the room with wonderful fragrance. You get the idea. When you practice gratitude you are giving your attention to what you have, whether it is connected with health or not, and it will result in a feeling of abundance. When you feel abundant you are giving off an abundant "vibe" and the Universe is listening.

If you want more joy and energy, gratitude is a crucial quality to cultivate. Gratitude comes from the heart and moves us out of limited thinking and fear into expansion and love. When we appreciate what we have we are making a direct connection with our soul and bringing our attention into the present moment, which is the only place that miracles can happen. You have read throughout this book how when I got out of my own way and appreciated what was going right in my life miracles happened for me. When we see with the eyes of the soul rather than through the eyes of ego the more our life comes into harmony with the healing power of the Universe and our Inner Physician. We are telling our Inner Physician that we appreciate its ability to heal and bring our body back into wellness. Research shows that consistently grateful people are happier, more energetic, more hopeful, more helpful, more empathic, more spiritual, more forgiving, and less materialistic. They're also less likely to be depressed, anxious, lonely, envious, neurotic, or sick. Grateful people tend to be more optimistic, a characteristic that researchers say boosts the immune system.

In one study by Dr. Sonja Lyubomirsky, one group of participants were asked to name five things they're grateful for every day, while another group was asked to list five hassles. Those expressing gratitude were not only happier and more optimistic, they reported fewer physical symptoms. Other gratitude studies have shown that those with chronic illnesses demonstrate clinical improvement when practicing regular gratitude.

Severely depressed people instructed to list grateful thoughts on a website daily were found to be significantly less depressed by the end of the study when compared to depressed people who weren't asked to express gratitude.

According to Dr. Lyubomirsky, gratitude:

1. Promotes savoring of positive life experiences

2. Bolsters self-worth and self-esteem

3. Helps people cope with stress and trauma

4. Encourages caring acts and moral behavior

5. Helps build social bonds, strengthen existing relationships, and nurture new relationships (and we know lonely people have twice the rate of heart disease as those with strong social connections)

6. Inhibits harmful comparisons

7. Diminishes or deters negative feelings such as anger, bitterness, and greed

8. Thwarts hedonistic adaptation (the ability to adjust your set point to positive new circumstances so that we don't appreciate the new circumstance and it has little effect on our overall health or happiness)

Dr. Christiane Northrup writes:

"The health benefits of gratitude, which is really the same thing as love, are an amazing example of just how sturdy the bridge is between the mind, body, and emotions. Research shows that heart-centered feelings associated with gratitude, appreciation, and caring are health enhancing. When you find one thing, however small, to be thankful for and you hold that feeling for as little as 15–20 seconds, many subtle and beneficial physiological changes take place in your body:

- *Stress hormone levels of cortisol and norepinephrine decrease, creating a cascade of beneficial metabolic changes such as an enhanced immune system.*

- *Coronary arteries relax, thus increasing the blood supply to your heart.*

- *Heart rhythm becomes more harmonious, which positively affects your mood and all other bodily organs.*

- *Breathing becomes deeper, thus increasing the oxygen level of your tissues."*

Other scientific evidence that gratitude improves health comes from research accumulated by Robert A. Emmons, professor of psychology at the University of California, Davis. Emmons found that gratitude makes you healthier, smarter, and more energetic. He also showed that people practicing gratitude daily, such as writing in a gratitude journal, reported higher levels of alertness, enthusiasm, determination, attentiveness, and energy than those who didn't."

In one study, they asked all participants to write a few sentences each week, focusing on particular topics.

One group wrote about things they were grateful for that had occurred during the week. A second group wrote about daily irritations or things that had displeased them, and the third wrote about events that had affected them (with no emphasis on them being positive or negative). After 10 weeks, those who wrote about gratitude were more optimistic and felt better about their lives. Surprisingly, they also exercised more and had fewer visits to physicians than those who focused on sources of aggravation.

Brain scans and research conducted by renowned psychiatrist Dr. Daniel Amen showed a significant improvement in brain function following the practice of gratitude. For years now, spiritual leaders and psychologists have claimed that a positive attitude can help heal our lives, but now we know that the simple act of gratitude can actually improve our physical and emotional well-being. And the cool thing is it's free and always available!

Let's explore some ways that you can add a practice of gratitude to your life and possibly speed up your return to wellness.

CREATIVE TECHNIQUE FOR WELLNESS

Cultivating Gratitude

Practice Makes Perfect

Cultivating gratitude, like maintaining strong muscles and bones, takes discipline and will, especially when you are not feeling well. Start each day with a grateful heart. It takes time to create a habit and even if you aren't doing it every day, what you are doing is helping. Here are a few suggestions for using gratitude to improve your attitude. Pick something that is easy for you to stay with:

1. Use gratitude to blot out unproductive feelings.

A lot of time during the healing journey, one can find that they are in a funk, feeling discouraged and wondering if things will ever change. We realize that we've lost our zest for life and a numb disinterest has taken its place. This is normal when we are not feeling well.

To turn this around, find something to be grateful for. Just one tiny thing is enough! Begin focusing on this thing as often as you can during the day, but most especially when that feeling of fear or doubt comes over you. Let a feeling of strong gratitude flood through your body, and you will shift to a more positive attitude almost immediately.

2. Begin expressing gratitude for the people around you each day.

Is a friend or family member getting on your nerves? Find one thing about him or her you can be grateful for, and focus all of your attention on that when you start to feel annoyed.

Remind yourself that everyone has both positive and negative personality traits – and you will encourage more displays of whatever you focus on! Focus on the positive traits of the people you encounter daily and watch as it transforms your interactions into mutually beneficial connections. Do you feel like you aren't getting enough support or encouragement from those around you? Do people avoid talking about your illness with you? Think of someone who has been supportive and focus your energy and gratitude on them and watch what happens.

3. Become an optimist with the help of gratitude.

Do you find yourself in the habit of always expecting the worst, fearing that you won't get better? When you become aware that you have shifted into a pessimistic mindset, consciously choose to shift into grateful optimism.

For example, if you catch yourself saying something like this, "I have been sick for so long it isn't possible that I will ever get better" – stop and turn that thought into something like, "I am feeling better and better each day. I am so grateful that I get to share another day with my family."

If you keep up with this practice even if it is just one time a day you should begin to see a big difference in your attitude and with that you will find that you are feeling more joy and happiness. You will begin to automatically notice more things to be grateful for.

4. Keep a gratitude journal.

I like to either buy a pretty journal or decorate a blank journal to use for my gratitude practice. Keep it by your bed and right before you go to bed write down the things that you are grateful for. At first your list might be short but as you continue you will find more and more things to be grateful for. Focus a few of those things on the progress you are making toward getting healthy. Over time you will be able to look back and see that you indeed are making progress.

As you write in your journal, challenge yourself by not repeating items from the previous days – this will make you look more deeply at all the little things that enhance your life and give you joy ... waking in a warm bed; your favorite song; a phone call from a friend; a great meal; the ability to touch, see, or hear; electricity; the beating of your heart; a hug; a butterfly you saw in the garden.

5. Write a thank you letter.

Write a thank you letter expressing gratitude for all the gifts of healing you have received from your Inner Physician. Talk as though it were a real person and get into as much detail about what you have received and how it made you feel. In studies of people who have written letters of gratitude to people the results are amazing.

While we may often thank people verbally, the written word can often be even more powerful because someone has taken the time to write their appreciation. A letter can also be re-read and treasured, creating joy and love that will continue to ripple out into the Universe.

6. Take a gratitude walk.

If you are well enough to go for a walk, this is a particularly useful practice when you're feeling down or filled with stress and worry. Set aside 20 minutes (or longer if you can) and walk in your neighborhood, through a park, around your office, or somewhere in nature.

As you walk, consider the many things for which you are grateful ... nurturing relationships, material comforts, the body that allows you to experience the world, the mind that allows you to really understand yourself, and your essential spiritual nature. Breathe, pause, and be grateful for the air that is filling your lungs and making your life possible.

Pay attention to your senses – everything you're seeing, hearing, feeling, smelling, and maybe even tasting – and see how many things you can find to feel grateful for. This is a powerful way to shift your mood and open to the flow of abundance that always surrounds you.

7. Express your gratitude regularly.

Every time you find something happening in your world that brings you joy say, "Thank you Universe, I want more!" or "Thank you God, send me more!"

8. Write an affirmation about your health.

Start your affirmation with, "I am so grateful and happy that I am feeling so healthy and energetic." Say it often.

You might even be able to think of some more things to do to practice gratitude. That's awesome!

AWAKENING YOUR INNER PHYSICIAN

It is said that it takes 28 days to create a new habit. Wouldn't it be great to have a habit of being grateful and appreciative about what we have?

Pick one of the activities from the list of ways to practice gratitude and do it consistently for 28 days. As an alternative you can pick four different activities and do each of them for a week. It doesn't matter what you are doing; it is more important that you are exercising your gratitude muscle.

Have fun with this and you will be surprised at what happens not only as you go along but by the time you have completed 28 days of this practice.

NOTE FROM THE AUTHOR

I humbly and gratefully present this book to the world and I feel a sense of vulnerability. I think this feeling is common especially for writers who write on a personal level. I am sharing deep parts of me and I don't know how it will be received but I am okay with that. I am sharing more about myself than most people know about me. And that is okay because my purpose in writing this is not to win some kind of award for being awesome, but to help people find that part of themselves that can help them heal. If I wasn't okay with what people thought after reading this book I couldn't let the baby go out into the world.

There is so much more I could have written about, so many other alternative techniques that can be used, but maybe in another book. The things I share are things that I had personal success with.

I want to express my gratitude to my readers. Thank you for being open to possibilities and taking this journey with me. I hope I have inspired you to think differently about wellness and disease. Remember that healing is a journey and everyone has their own process. Your journey will be completely different than mine or anyone else's. That is why it is important to learn how to tap into your Inner Physician.

Thank you to my Inner Physician for teaching me how miraculous and amazing my body is. Thank you for your patience when I wasn't listening. Thank you for showing me that when I was my own biggest obstacle there were other ways to get my attention. I am grateful that you pushed me to write this book.

I am grateful to my body for showing me so much about myself, things I would never have learned in any other way. Thank you for being strong, healthy and always returning to balance. Thank you for staying young as I age.

Thank you to all of those who have been on this journey with me, a list that is too long to mention here but you know who you are. I am truly grateful for everyone who has been a part of my life both in the short term and in the long term. I am a better person for your presence.

If one sentence, or one paragraph, a chapter or this entire book has an impact on someone's healing process in a positive way I am grateful. It is my wish for each of you if your body is currently out of balance that you return to perfect health and if you are currently healthy that you stay that way.

Blessings,

Katelyn Mariah
July 2014

If you have your own healing stories that you felt were miracles that were divinely guided either before you read this book or because you read this book and would like to share them please contact me through:

www.empoweredhealthandwellness.com

or email me at: magnetickatelyn@gmail.com.

Your Body Ecologist

Cutting-edge products for health and wellness:

There are many reputable companies out there but I recommend the following company for their high quality, cutting-edge products, and I know the owners and their high integrity and standards for excellence. These are the supplements that I choose for my body.

Are you looking for a product line that is set apart from others in the supplement field? You have found that with It Works! Global, who has created cutting-edge products with the highest quality ingredients. It Works! Global is a visionary company at the forefront of the ever-growing health and wellness distribution industry. So was I and that is why I chose to use these products to support my healthy lifestyle. I have personally tried every product in the line and use many of them daily.

It Works! Global has a first-to-market, body applicator that combines ancient herbal wisdom and sound scientific principles in a product that provides instant gratification, in tightening and toning as well as pain relief and reduction of inflammation. Many of the herbs are known for detoxifying. This is the herbal wrap I mentioned earlier in the book.

The It Works! Global vision, to provide you with one-of-a-kind, safe, effective, and affordable products, is driven by commitment to integrity at the forefront of their product development. It Works! Global products are formulated by leading scientists, herbalists, and researchers using the best natural ingredients, cutting-edge science, and strict quality standards to provide effective products that safely nourish your body and enhance your life.

An honest approach to nutrition and wholesome ingredients has guided It Works! Global through the harmonious blending of science and nature to bring superior, affordable products to your home. It Works! Global is proud to offer its one-of-a-kind body slimming treatments, top-notch nutritional supplements, and a specially-formulated skin care line that helps stop or delay the harmful environmental effects that contribute to the speed of the aging process.

It Works! Global supplements line is a comprehensive collection of nutritional solutions for real people like you to help you combat the elements and stay healthy. It Works! Global proudly stands behind their commitment to nutritional supplements that contain the highest quality ingredients, offering you real, life-changing results at affordable prices. Whether you're looking to reduce stress, lose weight, get top-notch nutrition, regulate your digestive system, or turn back the hands of time from the inside out, there is a solution for you in the It Works! Global supplement line.

Explore and order at www.YourBodyEcologist.com.

Soul Mandala Portraits for Healing

As you have read, art is very healing for the soul. A big part of my healing work over the years has been through art. I have created soul portraits for 100's of people over the years for all kinds of reasons. These portraits are created specifically with your healing intention in mind. Whatever issue you are working on will be the focus of the portrait.

Soul Mandala Portraits are personal spirit portraits created for you through a connection between your higher self and mine. You do not have to be in my presence because these images are coming from a fifth dimensional place and beyond. Through this connection your soul inspires me with information that your soul chooses as the best for your evolution at this time. The information comes through in image and is received at a higher level as you view it.

Each image contains coded information that is translated by the soul of the viewer. These codes of light impact the neurotransmitters in the brain, which translates the information and creates new pathways. Each image is designed to slowly stimulate and awaken the hidden unconscious receptors of the human mind to access coded information.

The codes of light in the images are the language of the Universe coming from pure Love. Each code is a package of information that will add to our awakening as they speak through the heart. The language of the heart, which is directly connected to the soul, is composed of forms, feelings, colors, shape and sound, not words. That is why when we open our hearts we are able to perceive and receive data transmissions through the images that expand our consciousness beyond the limitations of the mind and ego.

What this means is that you don't have to understand what you are looking at because the images bypass the mind and speak directly to your heart and soul. They can awaken dormant aspects within your DNA, helping you to align with your purpose. They hold and transmit vibrational frequencies that help bring change to your world. You will notice you are vibrating from a higher frequency after viewing these images. The images will speak directly to your Inner Physician and higher self.

Each portrait is an original water color painting that comes with a personal message for you. Cost is $111 and can be ordered at www.empoweredhealthandwellness.com.

Mystick Creek Essential Oils

I didn't mention essential oils in the book but want to leave it as a resource for your healing journey because they are so powerful and therapeutic. It has often been said that we have everything we need for support in life and in healing in nature. Whatever the issue there is something in nature that will help it come back into balance.

In addition to their intrinsic benefits to plants and being beautifully fragrant to people, essential oils have been used throughout history in many cultures for their medicinal and therapeutic benefits. Modern scientific study and trends toward more holistic approaches to wellness are driving a revival and new discovery of essential oil health applications.

Essential oils are multi-dimensional, filled with homeostatic intelligence to restore the body to a state of healthy balance. When body conditions change, oils adapt, raising or lowering blood pressure as needed, stimulating or repressing enzyme activity as needed, energizing or relaxing as needed. Oils have a natural intelligence.

Oil molecules send information to cells and cleanse receptor sites so that they bring your body back to natural function. Oils are balancing to the body. Oils address the causes of disease at a cellular level by deleting misinformation and reprogramming correct information so that cells function properly and in harmony with one another.

Because essential oils properly applied always work toward the restoration of proper bodily function, they do not cause undesirable side effects. They are feeding the body with truth and because of this they are a great adjunct therapy to use in your healing.

There are a lot of essential oils on the market and lots of books written about the properties of each oil so do some research on your particular issue and see what is suggested. I use dōTERRA oils to support my health and wellness because they are Certified Pure Therapeutic Grade oils and they are harvested in their natural habitat. This is important if you are to get the most effective results. Many oils are either synthetic or cut with synthetic oils so do your research.

dōTERRA CPTG Certified Pure Therapeutic Grade® essential oils represent the safest, purest, and most beneficial essential oils available today. They are gently and skillfully distilled from plants that have been patiently harvested at the perfect moment by experienced growers from around the world for ideal extract composition and efficacy. Experienced essential oil users will immediately recognize the superior quality standard for naturally safe, purely effective therapeutic-grade dōTERRA essential oils.

Explore dōTERRA here: www.mydoterra.com/470811/.

355

DIRECTORY OF
ALTERNATIVE RESOURCES

ALTERNATIVE HEALING

International Natural Healers Association
      www.internationalhealers.com
American Holistic Medical Association
      www.holisticmedicine.org

ART THERAPY

American Art Therapy Association
      www.arttherapy.com
Minnesota Art Therapy Association (Katelyn Mariah was a former president)
      www.mnata.org
Foundation for Art & Healing
      www.artandhealing.org/
Katelyn Mariah's Art Work/Soul Portraits
      www.empoweredhealthandwellness.com
      Email Katelyn Mariah magnetickatelyn@gmail.com

BREATH WORK

Holotropic Breath Work
    www.grof-holotropic-breathwork.net/
Breath Work Alliance
    www.breathworkalliance.com/
Rebirthing Breath work International
    Book: *The Miracle of the Breath: Mastering Fear, Healing Illness, and Experiencing the Divine* © 2005 by Andy Caponigro

CREATIVITY

American Creativity Association
    www.aca.cloverpad.org
National Coalition of Arts Therapies Associations
    www.nccata.org/
Center for Creative Arts
    www.creativeartstherapies.org/

DREAM WORK

International Association for the Study of Dreams
    www.asdream.org
Dreamwork Institute
    www.studioforthehealingarts.org

ESSENTIAL OILS FOR HEALING

Mystick Creek Essential Oils
   http://www.mydoterra.com/470811/

FREQUENCY SPECIFIC MICROCURRENT

   http://www.frequencyspecific.com/

HANDS-ON HEALING

Quantum Touch
   www.quantumtouch.com
Reiki - The International Center for Reiki Training
   www.reiki.org

HEALING TOUCH

Healing Touch International
   http://www.healingtouchinternational.org/

IMAGERY

Imagery International
   www.imageryinternational.org
International Imagery Association
   www.eidetictrainingcentertx.com/internationalimager
   yassociation

HEALTH AND WELLNESS SUPPLEMENTATION

www.YourBodyEcologist.com

METAPHORS FOR WELLBEING

Metaphors A-Z
    www.healingkeys.com
LOUISE HAY:
    Books: You Can Heal Your Life

MIND-BODY MEDICINE

Center for Mind-Body Medicine
    www.cmbm.org

RADIANT FREQUENCIES

Contact the author: Katelyn Mariah
magnetickatelyn@gmail.com

SHAMANISM

Society for Shamanic Practitioners
    www.shamansociety.org
LUZCLARA Chilean Light Worker
    www.luzclara.com

Americo Yabar
    www.salkawasi.eu
Dhyani Ywahoo
    www.sunray.org

SOUND HEALING

Jonathan Goldman's Sound Healing
    www.healingsounds.com
Sound Healers Association
    www.soundhealersassociation.org
Sound Health Options
    www.soundhealthoptions.com

AUTHORS MENTIONED
IN THE BOOK

Allen, James: As A Man Thinketh

Amen, Daniel: http://www.amenclinics.com

Bell, Bonnie and David Todd: Gaia Star Mandalas

Braden, Gregg: www.greggbraden.com

Brennan, Barbara: www.barbarabrennan.com

     Barbara Brennan School of Healing

Brofman, Martin: http://www.healer.ch/Foundation.html

     The Brofman Foundation for the Advancement of Healing

Cherry, Kendra: The Everything Psychology Book

Chopra, Deepak: www.deepakchopra.com

     Chopra Center for Wellbeing: www.chopra.com

Emmons, Robert A.: http://gratitudepower.net/science.htm

Emoto, Masaru: www.masaru-emoto.net

Estes, Clarissa Pinkola: www.clarrisapinkolaestes.com

Hay, Louise: www.louisehay.com

Hicks, Esther: www.abraham-hicks.com

Lyubomirsky, Sonja: http://sonjalyubomirsky.com

Northrup, Christiane: www.drnorthrup.com

Osho: http://www.oshostore-sedona.com

Robbins, Tony: www.tonyrobbins.com

Simeona, Morrnah and Dr. Hew Len: www.self-identity-through-hooponopono.com

Tedlock, Barbara: www.barbaratedlock.com

The Secret: www.thesecret.tv

Vitale, Joe: www.zerolimits.com

SYMBOLS USED IN THE BOOK

 **SEED OF LIFE:** The seed of life pattern is made of seven interlocking circles. Some beliefs see these seven circles as the seven days in which God created life. First one circle was created and on each further day another circle was added. Once all seven circles were formed the seed of life was born. And from this shape the flower of life (which is basically like the seed of life but with another layer of circles around the outside) is built, which contains the blueprint of the Universe. Therefore all that exists can be built from the seed of life. The oldest version of this can be seen in the Temple of Osiris at Abydos. All things existing can be built from the shape of the seed of life. I chose this symbol because we all have a blueprint for health that the Inner Physician is following as it brings us back to perfect balance in wellness.

 **HUMMINGBIRD:** Hummingbird has a lot of symbolic meanings including joy. Another symbolic meaning of the hummingbird is its ability to accomplish the impossible. Even if the hummingbird is one of the smallest birds, it can travel great distances, sometimes 2000 miles. Those who have that bird as their totem are characterized by their resiliency and their ability to run great distances tirelessly. Inspired by this

totem, you will be inclined to accomplish what seems impossible to most while keeping it light and enjoyable.

The hummingbird is known for burning a lot of energy quickly to keep flying and therefore needs to find sources of food constantly. If you have the hummingbird as a totem, you may benefit from resting often and taking time to feed yourself with enough, whether it's physically, emotionally or spiritually, to keep going.

In the Andes of South America the hummingbird is a symbol of resurrection. It seems to die on cold nights, but comes back to life again at sunrise.

 **TRIPLE SPIRAL/TRISKELE:** This triple spiral /the spiral of life is an ancient symbol of the Celts. They believed that all life moved in eternal cycles, regenerating at each juncture. If you look at the sign carefully, you will notice that it is drawn in one single line without a beginning or an end, suggesting a continuous movement of time.

The Celts also believed that all important things came in three phases such as birth/death/rebirth, or mind/body/spirit. The three spirals represent balance, harmony and continual motion of the flow of life and of the Earth's seasons and cycles.

This symbol is a reflection of our existence and the truth of our nature of being. We often try to perceive present occurrences from one point of view when the present is a "hair's breadth" of a moment, which was the future a moment ago and is already becoming the past. This symbol reinforces the movement and interconnection between the dimensions or realms of consciousness, ordinary reality, the underworld and higher worlds, all integral to a complete earth experience, meaning we are connected to higher wisdom, God, Angels and our Inner Physician in our search for wellness.

ABOUT THE AUTHOR

Katelyn Mariah BFA, MA, LICSW is a visionary artist and expressive arts therapist with training in art therapy, sandplay therapy and play therapy. She studied fine arts at The Minneapolis College of Art and Design and the University of Minnesota, where she earned a Bachelor of Fine Arts Degree. She received a Master's Degree from St. Mary's University in Winona, Minnesota, with an emphasis in Art, Art Therapy, and Child Abuse. She has Professional and Advanced training from the Center for Mind-Body Medicine.

Katelyn's career as psychotherapist spanned 26 years before she retired to pursue a career in Health and Wellness. Using the combined gifts of art and psychotherapy she worked with children at risk of abuse and neglect and with families. Katelyn served as the president of The Minnesota Art therapy Association for a two-year term and on the Board of the Minnesota Sandplay Therapy Group for a three-year term.

Katelyn designed and developed a therapeutic game for children to explore and express healthy anger called Angry Animals, and created a spiritual meditation deck called Awaken the Goddess.

Katelyn's art has been visionary for the last 25 years and is an expression of her transformation and connection to Spirit. She has been on a path of personal transformation for 30 years and has studied shamanic traditions around the world. She has studied with a shaman from Peru, a Cherokee lineage holder, a teacher in Hawaii and a medicine woman in Chile.

Katelyn has been a student of metaphysics for many years. Her studies include the writings of Rudolf Steiner, Tibetan teachings, mythology, numerology, Law of Attraction and other metaphysical subjects as well as alternative health and nutrition. She studied sound healing with internationally known sound healer Jonathan Goldman. Katelyn has traveled to Mexico, Canada, Chile, Austria and Bali to further both her art career and her spiritual studies.

She is the mother of two adult children, Nathan and Carrie, and grandmother to Goma. She lives in St. Paul, Minnesota.

Katelyn can be contacted through her website, www.empoweredhealthandwellness.com.